# Garden Flowers

# A CONCISE GUIDE IN COLOUR

# Garden Flowers

*by Vlastimil Vaněk*

*Illustrated*

*by František Severa*

*Hamlyn*

*London • New York • Sydney • Toronto*

Translated by Daniela Coxon
Designed and produced by Artia for
THE HAMLYN PUBLISHING GROUP LIMITED
London ● New York ● Sydney ● Toronto
Hamlyn House, Feltham, Middlesex, England
Copyright © 1971 by Artia
Reprinted 1972, 1973

ISBN 0 600 33852 5

Printed in Czechoslovakia
3/02/11-51

# CONTENTS

# INTRODUCTION

Flowers are an essential part of a garden which would seem bare and deserted without them. They are the main source of colour and beauty, and can give pleasure from the earliest spring to late autumn.

But it is not only flowers which make a garden. We should soon tire of them without the contrast of open and peaceful stretches of green lawn. The flowers, important as they are, are only a part of the garden; shrubs and trees, whether coniferous or deciduous, also play a major part. They give the garden a spatial framework. They can be used to hide incongruous corners and to separate off some parts of the garden to give privacy. Groups of shrubs, in particular the conifers, provide an excellent dark background for the luminescence of flowers; they make their shapes stand out.

There is a great choice of suitable flowers for the garden. The beginner often does not know what to choose from the vast array of species and varieties in gardening catalogues. It is necessary to have a certain amount of knowledge to choose the most suitable types. The characteristics of the main groups of flowers with their advantages and disadvantages are briefly listed below.

The main charm of annuals is the rich colour of their flowers and the long flowering period of some species. Summer is their main flowering time. Some of them are very suitable for cutting, while others are superbly suited to low, colourful lay-outs. But these advantages are limited by a major disadvantage: annuals have a short life as they die off in autumn, and must be renewed every year. Quite a lot of work is involved in planting out every year, especially if gardeners want to raise their own seedlings.

Biennials have the same disadvantages; they have to be replaced in the same way as annuals. Their life lasts two years; in the first year they usually form only the foliage and after flowering in the second year, they die away.

Bulbous and tuberous plants form another separate group. Bulbs have their main flowering period in spring, sometimes as early as February. They produce a whole range of lively colours, and are, perhaps, incomparable in this respect. But their beauty is offset by a great disadvantage: they flower for a relatively short time, mostly two to three weeks, and after fading away they 'shrivel up', when the leaves turn yellow, become dry and die away leaving seemingly empty places in the garden. Only the bulbs and tubers live on in the ground.

In Britain bulbs are used extensively to provide interest and colour before other plants have started to grow, and are particularly suitable for places where a rich colourful effect is wanted, perhaps for only a short time.

Perennials form the last group. They are flowers which have none of the disadvantages of the three previous groups for the grower, yet are equally rich in shape and colour. In addition they live longer, so it is unnecessary to renew and plant them every year.

The choice of perennials is very wide and covers plants with a flowering period extending from the earliest spring to the onset of frost and with different environmental needs. One of the many advantages of perennials is the fact that they can be planted in both normal and extreme conditions. There are types which thrive in hot, dry conditions, while others are suitable for damp conditions, half-shade or full shade. It only needs a careful selection to ensure that the garden will be in flower almost all the year round. And even in winter it need not be bare; many perennials have beautiful, evergreen leaves which, in colour and shape, give pleasure even while snow is on the ground.

It is the aim of this book to help the gardener in his effort to keep the garden in flower throughout most of the year and give him advice on where, how and what to grow so that his garden will be full of colour and beauty and a continual source of pleasure.

# The growth and care of perennials

If perennials are provided with suitable conditions at the start, they usually require very little care. Good preparation of the soil before planting and a choice of suitable types are important. The types which prefer half-shade and dampness will not thrive in full sunshine and dryness, and vice versa.

The majority of perennials are not particularly demanding as to the quality of the soil and are, in the main, content with the soil to be found in the average garden. This is a medium loam with plenty of humus. At all events it should be neither too dense nor too permeable. Heavy, impermeable, or wet and cold soils are less suitable. It is essential to improve such types of soil before planting perennials (and also other plants) by adding peat, sand and, most important, well-matured compost.

Sandy soil is the opposite of heavy, compact ground. It does not retain moisture well, it dries out easily and some types of perennials then suffer from drought. The problem is solved by adding heavier soil and peat, which has a high rate of water retention and holds water in the soil. That is why a good peat is a common material for improving the physical nature of the soil: it aerates and makes heavy soils lighter and moisturizes light soils.

Care must be taken in providing a good soil before planting, as the majority of perennials are sensitive to fresh manure. A good, aged, decomposed, nourishing compost is always the most suitable material. Fresh, unrotted manure is entirely unsuitable, as are artificial feeds, which damage young plants and cuttings. If artificial feeds are used, they should be added to the soil at least a month before planting to allow them to be absorbed and to soften their burning effect on roots. If manure is used, it is best to use a well-rotted farmyard type.

Some forethought must be given to the improvement of the soil, as certain types of perennials prefer a soil that is poorer and less nourishing. In a soil that is too rich they become overgrown; the foliage is rank and the plants often flower little and die out easily. Examples of this sort of plant are the low-growing species of Yarrow or Milfoil *(Achillea)*, Alyssum *(Alyssum montanum* and *A. saxatile)*, Stonecrop *(Sedum)*, Thyme *(Thymus)* and, indeed, the majority of low-growing rockery plants. For these types a rather sandy soil mixed with rubble should be prepared.

In contrast, good feeding and preparation of the soil are necessary for some plants more rigorous in their requirements, such as Bear's Breeches *(Acanthus)*, Japanese Anemone *(Anemone japonica)*, Columbine *(Aquilegia)*, Astilbe *(Astilbe)*, Delphinium *(Delphinium)*, Bleeding Heart *(Dicentra)*, Foxtail Lily *(Eremurus)*, 'Bristol Fairy', 'Flamingo' *(Gypsophila paniculata)*, Hellebore *(Helleborus)*, Sneezeweed *(Helenium)*, Day Lily *(Hemerocallis)*, Plantain Lily *(Hosta)*, all types of Chrysanthemums, Lupin *(Lupinus)*, Paeony *(Paeonia)*, Phlox *(Phlox paniculata)*, Primula *(Primula)*, etc.

During the preparation of the soil before planting perennials, very careful weeding is really important. If bits of rhizomes or weed roots remain in the soil, they spread so much that they soon overrun the flowers. Perennials remain in one place for several years and, as the soil is not turned over for a long time, the roots of the weeds have plenty of time to develop. It is not usually possible to destroy them by digging in between the plants. That is why careful preparation of the soil before planting will always be worthwhile.

In connection with this, soil reaction should be mentioned, at least briefly. There are alkaline soils originating from slate or limestone, neutral soils with a primary rock foundation and acid soils, originating from a perpetually wet base. The majority of perennials which are described in this book thrive well in alkaline and neutral soils. The selection does not completely exclude types which cannot stand lime in the soil, even though *Anemone japonica* and *Astilbe*, for instance, are better off in a soil which is not too calcareous. But for many species an adequate amount of humus and moisture is much more important. Each plant's specific requirements are stated as it is described.

Where some perennials require half-shade, such shading as is afforded by thin trees or shrubs, or possibly a house, is most suitable. However, the choice of tree is important, for although providing the right amount of shelter, some trees dehydrate the soil so much that hardly any of the perennials grow well beneath them. The birch tree is an example; only drought-loving plants can survive in its shade.

When the soil has been prepared (weeded, well tilled, improved by the addition of humus and raked), the gardener can start planting out. It is possible to plant perennials nearly all year round, but the most suitable periods are in early spring or early autumn. A pattern has been established whereby those species which flower in spring are planted in autumn, and those which flower in summer or in autumn are planted out in spring. If the young plants are pot- or container-grown, the time of planting is not crucial. The spring period from about mid-March until the end of April is the best, as the soil then has a sufficient amount of natural moisture; the weather is usually milder but not too hot, it rains more often and the air is moister. These are all factors very favourable to the quick rooting of seedlings.

Autumn planting is usually started in September with the aim of finishing by about the middle of October. It is important for plants to have rooted well by winter, otherwise the frost may dislodge an inadequately rooted plant, the roots are torn and the whole plant often becomes seriously damaged. This mainly applies to shallow-rooting types. It is

12

therefore advisable for late plantings in winter to be well covered by chopped bracken, coniferous cuttings or sacking which provide a protection against the frost.

If the young plants have come from a nursery, it is useful to heel them into the soil before finally planting them out so that an overall impression can be gained and then they can be planted according to a prepared plan. For this it is useful to set aside part of a well-tilled flower-bed somewhere in the shade. After the young plants have been unwrapped they should be sprayed with water and put in the prepared flower-bed, then their roots should be covered with soil and marked with name-cards. Afterwards the heeled-in plants should be watered again. They can be left like that for several days and can be replanted later at leisure according to the prepared plan.

It is essential to trim the plants before bedding them, to shorten long roots and parts above the ground, except when plants are pot-grown and have developed firm root balls. These can be planted at any time of the year without risk, even when they are flowering.

Before planting it is first necessary to measure out the flower-beds and mark out the area to be planted. It is also necessary to ensure that the soil is moist. If conditions are dry, the beds should be watered a day or so before planting. It is important that individual plants are not planted too close together. Low, undemanding varieties are planted fairly close together at intervals of 20—30 cms (8—12 ins), medium-sized plants at intervals of about 40 cms (16 ins) and larger plants are put in at intervals of approximately 60—100 cms (2—3 ft). The distances, which are specified in this book in the individual entry for each plant, should not be under-estimated as the plants should have plenty of space to develop properly. But, on the other hand, they should not be planted too thinly. Empty spaces between established plants do not look very attractive. A hole should be dug for each plant large enough for the roots to fit in comfortably without being cramped and the roots then covered with soil and pressed firmly down. After planting, the plants should be given a good watering. The depth of planting should ensure that the new shoot buds are level with the ground surface. Some species cannot stand deeper planting. If the weather is dry, they should be watered several times.

After planting is finished it is useful to top dress the ground between the plants with a layer of peat about 3—5 cms (1—2 ins) deep. This layer retains the soil's moisture quite well and prevents the ground surface from getting lumpy. Later on when the peat is mixed into the ground during digging, it has a beneficial effect on the physical composition of the soil. If no peat is available it is useful to fork the surface of the soil lightly now and then, as it helps to keep the soil moist, prevent the formation of a crust and destroy germinating weeds.

During the year the earth between perennial plants should occasionally be hoed and the flower-beds weeded carefully. As soon as the plants are stronger and big enough to cover the soil entirely, weeds cannot grow any more and so digging around them is no longer necessary. It is important to hoe around the older growths more often, especially in spring. They should be watered from time to time, especially during dry periods, either with a hose or a garden spray. Occasionally it is necessary to feed the more demanding types. For winter the plants should be given a top dressing of good, nourishing compost, if need be the peat quick-compost; and during the course of the year, especially in the period of the greatest growth in spring and early summer, they should be fed with a liquid manure.

The source of compost is primarily humus, which is important not only for its nutritious contents, but also in terms of soil bacterias and other micro-organisms. But it is difficult to get good compost and so it is useful if the gardener can make it himself. First a suitable place in the garden must be found. The compost heap should be in the shade, so if possible it should be somewhere under trees, and it should also be readily accessible so that all the necessary ingredients can be supplied easily. Piped water should be near at hand as watering the compost is very important. As a compost heap is not a star attraction, it is usually placed somewhere apart and camouflaged by hedges or a group of other larger plants.

Nearly all organic waste from the house and the garden is suitable for compost. For example vegetable peelings and various other left-overs from the kitchen, weeds, turf and dead leaves can all be used. Weeds with ripe seeds and rotten fruit and similar material, which can become a source of contagious disease, are unsuitable. This material should be piled up in layers about 20 cms (8 ins) deep, sprayed with water and covered with a layer of earth 5—10 cms (2—4 ins) deep. These layers should not be piled to a height of more than 1 metre (3 ft) at the most. The sides of the mound are angled at 45°. The top is depressed a little for easier watering. If the waste is mixed with powdered lime or with nitro-chalk when piling it up, the decomposition of the organic material is accelerated and the compost is usually ready to be used after only one year. Otherwise the maturation of compost takes at least two years. To prevent dehydration of the compost, it is necessary to cover the pile with a layer of peat about 10 cms (4 ins) deep. Then the compost is left to mature and during dry or warm weather it should be watered periodically, if possible with dung water. If a few holes are made at the top with a pointed stake, the liquid will filter down to the lower layers more effectively and more quickly.

If lime or nitro-chalk are added during construction the pile can be dug over in four to five months and re-arranged. In this way the compost is aerated and mixed. Then it is covered with peat again and left to mature. The compost is usually ready after several more months, when the whole mound has a homogeneous soily structure and the original material is no longer identifiable. If the compost is not yet in such a state, it is left to mature further.

But if this is too long to wait and plenty of peat is available, a so-called peat quick-compost can easily be made in the following manner:

Mix 1 bale or 70 kilograms (140 pounds) of peat with 7 kilograms (14 pounds) of one of the standard products to aid quick rotting available under various trade names, 7 kilograms (14 pounds) of sulphate of potash and 5 kilograms (10 pounds) of nitro-chalk. Mix it well, moisten with water (about 250 litres [50 gallons]) and pile up into a compost shape. Cover it with a layer of earth 10—15 cms (4—6 ins) deep and leave it to rest. After about four weeks shift the compost and cover it again with soil. After another four weeks the fertilizers in the peat are decomposed and absorbed to such an extent that the compost can be used. The specified quantity will be sufficient to fertilize an area of 100—150 square metres (300—450 square yards). This peat compost enriches the soil mainly with nutriments and humus and physically improves it.

It is necessary to feed free-growing plants during the year and most suitable for this is a fertilizer which can be added in liquid form. It is prepared by dissolving a balanced full garden feed in water. To 10 litres (2 gallons) of water add about one or two tablespoons of feed. This solution can be poured straight on to the roots. Some types are sensitive to their leaves being sprayed with liquid feed and therefore the leaves should be sprayed afterwards with water. When the plants are fully grown, feeding can be repeated several times at fortnightly intervals. On principle feeds are not given to plants which thrive better in a rather poorer soil, such as some of the low-growing rock plants mentioned earlier.

Perennials usually do not need any other attention during the year. Dead flowerheads should be removed as they usually do not look very decorative, and a second crop of flowers is thereby encouraged. In autumn, before the cold weather sets in, the foliage should be trimmed to a height of about 10 cms (4 ins) above the ground, with the exception of those leaves which remain green throughout the winter. Autumn plantings, which did not manage to root sufficiently, should be covered. Otherwise only the more sensitive plants are given a protective covering such as Japanese Anemone *(Anemone japonica)*, Sun Rose *(Helianthemum)*, *Incarvillea*, Red Hot Poker *(Kniphofia)*, *Macleaya*, *Miscanthus*, *Rodgersia*. *Miscanthus* should always be cut back in spring and before winter its basal growth should be protected from frost with a layer of dead leaves. *Eremurus* should be protected with leaves and on top of this a piece of PVC foil to prevent it getting wet in winter as it will not tolerate damp.

Twigs or spruce cuttings are the most suitable material for winter covering, as they are airy and seem to deter mice. In spring, mainly at the beginning of March, when the danger of stronger frosts is over, the coverings can gradually be removed.

As soon as the soil dries out sufficiently, the ground between the plants should be hoed, and a little compost or peat quick-compost dug in if necessary.

# The propagation of perennials

Perennials multiply in various ways and the gardener's main concern is, given that the conditions are right, to choose the easiest and the surest way. In principle there are two main ways of propagation, by seed (generatively) and by cuttings or by division (vegetatively).

It is most natural for plants to set seed, but in fact it is not easy to raise all plants from seed. This requires certain technical equipment (hotbed, bowls, boxes, etc.) which is quite elaborate and even the experienced gardener does not

17

always manage to achieve really good results. Even when sturdy plants are cultivated from seed, their characteristics are not always true to the parent plant.

The quality of plants propagated from seed depends on the degree of their hybridization. Botanical and natural species give good results on the whole and young plants usually do not differ from parent plants. But the more improved the plant is, especially through crossbreeding, the more likely the plants from home-gathered seed will not conform to the parent. For this reason hybrids resulting from crossbreeding are propagated vegetatively. If some multiply vegetatively with difficulty or if it is only possible to propagate them from seed, then their selection is important so that they give as good a result as possible.

For instance Columbines *(Aquilegia)*, Foxgloves *(Digitalis)*, Blanket Flowers *(Gaillardia)*, Pyrethrums *(Chrysanthemum roseum)*, Russell Lupins *(Lupinus Russell hybrids)*, Primulas *(Primula elatior, P. acaulis, P. denticulata)* and Violas or Horned Pansies *(Viola cornuta)* can be propagated from seed and give good results only when improved seed is used which has been especially prepared and selected by a seed merchant. If seed developed without improvement techniques (selection, isolation, etc.) is used, there is no guarantee that a good quality plant will be produced.

But there are types which always give quality offspring from seed. They are usually natural forms which are only changed a little by selection, for instance Monkshood *(Aconitum)*, Pheasant's Eye *(Adonis)*, Madwort *(Alyssum)*, Soapwort *(Saponaria ocymoides)*, 'Bristol Fairy', 'Flamingo' *(Gypsophila paniculata)*, Lavender *(Lavandula)*, Flax *(Linum)*, Evening Primrose *(Oenothera)*, Globe Thistle *(Echinops)*, Foxtail Lily *(Eremurus)*, etc.

Some specimens in specific varieties multiply vegetatively, but propagation is sometimes difficult or does not produce a sufficient quantity of young plants. The variety is propagated therefore from seed even at the cost of the young plants not conforming exactly to the parents. But they are usable, and the advantages of propagation by seed will compensate for any disadvantages of slight variability. For example this applies to Michaelmas Daisy *(Aster amellus)*, Delphinium *(Delphinium)*, Pink *(Dianthus plumarius)*, Ox-eye Daisy *(Chrysanthemum leucanthemum)* and Russell Lupin, among others.

The sowing of the majority of perennials is carried out in spring, usually from March to April in a cold or semi-warm cold-frame, or in bowls or boxes. A small quantity of seed can be sown in flower-pots. The earth for sowing should be light, sandy, permeable, completely healthy and free from germs of various diseases, mould-free, etc. A mixture of leaf-mould or peat with good garden soil and sand (in a ratio of about 2:2:1) is suitable or John Innes Potting Compost No. 1 or one of the soilless mediums now on the market. Good drainage in the seeding bowl is important. First of all the bottom of the flower-pot or bowl should be covered with a layer of coarse sand several centimetres deep and on top of this some of the soil mixture used for sowing should be scattered; after it has been pressed down lightly, it is ready for sowing. Great care must be taken not to sow too thickly, especially with fine seed which germinates readily. Then the seed is sprinkled with a thin layer of clean, sieved sharp sand and lightly pressed again. After this it is watered carefully so that the sown seed does not float away. A very fine rose or mist sprayer should, therefore, be used for watering and only as much water given as will seep through. It must never remain on the surface. The bowls and flower-pots are then inserted in the cold-frame and covered with glass. On sunny days they should be shaded and ventilated.

When the seeds start coming up, they should be aired for longer periods. The young plants are transplanted, when they are strong enough, either to boxes or direct to the cold-frame. They are usually pricked out in boxes at intervals of $2-3$ cms ($\frac{3}{4}-1\frac{1}{4}$ ins) and in cold-frames $6-8$ cms ($2\frac{1}{2}-3\frac{1}{2}$ ins) apart. As soon as the seedlings root and gain a little strength, the glass covers should be removed and they should be allowed to harden off gradually. Many types can be transplanted directly to a well-prepared, protected and slightly shady flower-bed, where they remain until they are moved to their final positions.

Some species benefit a lot from their seeds being frozen; in fact some do not germinate without this, for instance, the Globe Flowers *(Trollius)*. Freezing can considerably increase the successful germination of Monkshood *(Aconitum)*, Pheasant's Eye *(Adonis) Brunnera*, Burning Bush *(Dictamnus)*, Foxtail Lily *(Eremurus)*, Hellebore *(Helleborus)* , Day Lily *(Hemerocallis)*, etc.

Some species, which have biennial characteristics, are sown at the end of spring, when they develop more quickly, for the gardener's aim is to cultivate sufficiently strong plants by autumn to withstand the winter. These species are sown at the beginning of June; in this group, for instance, are Foxglove *(Digitalis)* and Mullein *(Verbascum)*. Under good conditions the plants develop so that it is possible to bed them out even during September, and they then flower in the second year. This also applies to Wallflowers *(Cheiranthus)*, Stocks *(Mathiola)* and Sweet Williams *(Dianthus barbatus)*.

Propagation by vegetative means is based on the division of plants: either by direct division of the old plant clumps, by removing suckers and planting these, or by dividing the roots. The most suitable method depends on the growth of individual forms.

The division of old plants is the easiest method of propagation and it can be used with the majority of types. The clump should be carefully lifted from the soil, the surplus soil shaken off, and then split into several well-rooted pieces. The most vigorous and best pieces are found round the edge of the plant and, if possible, they alone should be used. The upper parts and roots should be shortened a little and if the pieces are strong enough, they can be planted straight away in an appropriate place. If it is necessary to produce a greater number of young plants and in so doing divisions are smaller, the new plants should be planted more closely in the flower-bed and when they are strong enough they should be re-positioned.

The suitable time for the division and replanting of perennials differs in different genera of plants. Spring (March or April) is more suitable for some types, while for others, the end of summer or early autumn is better. An approximate rule is that perennials flowering in spring are divided in autumn, while those flowering in summer and in autumn are divided in spring, but many can be divided in this way in both seasons. In Britain it is nearly all done in autumn.

Cuttings are taken to propagate those perennials which form roots easily. This provides more young plants from one parent plant than division. The minimum equipment required is a cold-frame, as cuttings root best under glass. Autumn and spring are the main propagating seasons, the time when plants bud and root.

Stems are used as cuttings and these should be cut into lengths of about 4—6 cms (1½—2½ ins). The lower leaves together with the petioles should be cut away and the top leaves shortened by about a third. The cuttings, trimmed in this way, are then planted in clean, sharp sand or in a mixture of sand and peat either straight into a cold-frame or into bowls and flower-pots. They should then be covered with glass frames and shaded, and by watering with a fine rose or spray a constant mild dampness can be maintained. They should be given more air and light as soon as the cuttings begin to root. The easiest begin to root after a week (Stonecrop, for example) but usually it takes 2—4 weeks, and sometimes even longer depending on the plant. Then the young rooted plants should be placed either in a cold-frame or in a well-prepared flower-bed, as with young seedlings, to finish growing.

Some perennials are propagated by root cuttings which

have longer, pulpy roots capable of forming adventitious buds.

In autumn, before the soil freezes, this type of plant should be carefully removed from the ground so that their long roots are damaged as little as possible. The stronger and healthier roots should be cut out in small bunches, marked and placed in damp sand in a cellar or similar cool, dark place. Then early in spring these roots can be cut into pieces 4—5 cms ($1\frac{1}{2}$—2 ins) long and put, slightly at a slant, in boxes (be sure the top parts of the roots are upwards!) in a mixture of mature cold-frame soil and sand. The upper parts of the cuttings must be covered with a layer of soil about 1 cm ($\frac{3}{8}$ in.) deep. The boxes should then be replaced in a cellar or in a cold-frame. It is better to transplant the young plants after rooting into flower-pots and rear them there. Usually they are ready to be planted out after one year.

# Perennials for every season

Gardens, like everything else around us, are constantly developing. Looking at the history of gardens through the centuries, it is apparent how the style of their arrangement has changed and, with these changes in style, even the way of employing flowers has altered. Modern thinking is gradually moving away from the regular shapes of formal flower-beds and passing on to freer, natural shapes. The elaborately kept parterres and gravel walks have been replaced by paths of natural stone, which are more easily maintained, and the geometrically regular flower-beds by free groups of flowers, which give a more natural impression and bring out more fully the beauty of perennials. Striking colour is no longer the gardener's chief aim and the subtle beauty of different shades of green and grey foliage is beginning to be appreciated.

Gardens are no longer overstocked with flowering plants; instead, flowers are used sparingly and planted with large areas of grass as contrast, so that the groups of flowers stand out more clearly. Decorative types of grass are also beginning to be appreciated; in addition to their delicate foliage, which provides a welcome contrast to heavier leaves and a good foil to groups of flowers, they are, moreover, beautiful all the year round.

It is not the aim of the modern gardener to assemble the largest number of species and varieties of flowers. On the contrary, he prefers to work with a smaller assortment, but to choose each type with care and place it carefully.

In order to combine perennials together harmoniously and to take full advantage of their beauty, their colours, period of bloom and also their height must be borne in mind. Apart from this, it is also necessary to respect the requirements of individual species as to the quality of the soil (especially in dry and damp conditions) and the amount of light necessary. Species which have similar requirements are combined together. When drawing up a planting scheme, it is useful to have at hand a summary of perennials listed according to their requirements and with detailed directions as to how individual types of perennials can be used.

Each season of the year is characterized by certain flowers peculiar to it, but the flowers of early spring have a particular charm. The first signs of spring, after a long, hard winter, are eagerly awaited and the first bloom, often while the snow is still on the ground, has an immense appeal. Only the hardiest species flower in early spring, such as Hellebores and *Adonis amurensis* together with Snowdrops; the most precocious are the dwarf Irises *(Iris danfordiae* and *I. reticulata)* and *Daphne mezereum*, which come into flower in February and at the beginning of March.

Early spring (the period from March to April) is richer in blooms. The earliest Primulas *(Primula denticulata, P. rosea, P. acaulis)*, Blue-eyed Mary and the early bulbous plants, particularly Crocuses and some of the earliest species of Tulips, begin to flower, and introduce patches of lively colour into the garden.

Spring which in terms of the garden extends from mid-April until the end of May, is a period when an immense wealth of flowers of various shapes and hues suddenly bursts into flower. Bulbous plants are fully in flower, especially Daffodils, Hyacinths, *Muscari*, Bluebells, Tulips and many others. In this time of prodigious growth the perennials are mainly represented by various low, creeping varieties, such as Madwort, most of the Primulas, Perennial Candytuft and many others, which belong rather to rockeries. In rockeries and in formal flower-beds of low-growing species it is the richest period of blossom. Among the first of the taller species to come into flower are Bleeding Heart, Leopard's Bane, Globe Flower, *Epimedium* and Spurge.

Some of the taller perennials are in full flower by early summer, which lasts from the end of May until the beginning of July. It is a period of blue Delphiniums, flashing red Poppies, brilliant Columbines, Lupins of all colours and decorative Irises and Paeonies, which occupy an important place among perennials. Lavender-blue Catmint is in full bloom, making a beautiful contrast with Catchfly and all the other plants in flower at the same time.

Hot summer in July and August also has its typical representatives. First there are the familiar and popular Ox-eye Daisies, which together with Blanket Flowers make the garden shimmer. At this time Goat's Beard reigns in damp and half-shaded gardens. In the second part of the summer the garden is completely flooded with Coneflowers, Phloxes and Sneezeweeds. Some of the low-growing perennials do not have a long flowering period which is why the Evening Primrose, Campion and Viola, which flower continuously from May onwards, are so valuable to the gardener.

Early autumn (September) is still rich in blossoms. Blue,

24

pink and red Michaelmas Daisies, golden-yellow Golden Rod, Sunflowers, some of the Stonecrops, delicate Japanese Anemones and purple Monkshood form the contents of the flower-beds at this time. Early Chrysanthemums also start flowering. The leaves of some types of perennials and shrubs begin to change colour and the garden is gay with the coloured fruits of flowers such as Chinese Lantern and, above all, of trees and shrubs.

In late autumn (October and November) nature gradually starts to prepare for its winter rest. Blossoms are few, but Chrysanthemums, a few late Michaelmas Daisies, late varieties of Anemones and the tireless Evening Primrose are still in flower.

The flowering season slowly comes to a close and perennials remain the only decoration in the garden; the leaves of ever-green species make the garden appear less dead and barren and looking to the future, the gardener should not forget to include some in his planting scheme. An assortment could include, for instance, Perennial Candytuft, Megasea, grey-leaved Madwort, Bugle, Speedwell, Day Lily, Sun Rose, Thyme, etc.

# Different ways of using perennials

The formal herbaceous flower-bed is one of the oldest and most well-tried ways of planting perennials, even though it is the practice to refrain more and more from employing regular flower-beds.

The herbaceous border or island flower-bed can be of various shapes and sizes, both regular and irregular, acces-sible from one or two sides, and is therefore designed accordingly. At first sight the herbaceous border is the easiest way of planting, but designing the planting of such a flower-bed to make it well balanced in both colour and shape, to have it in flower all the time and to make it decorative all year round, is quite exacting work, which presupposes a knowledge of types and varieties and considerable good taste.

The herbaceous border is usually sited in the garden along-side a path and, perhaps, near a garden seat, from where it is possible to observe the effect in peace and comfort. The beauty of a well-designed flower-bed stands out especially well if it has a suitable background. This can be a hedge, the peaceful green colouring of which outlines the flowers, or a pergola or trellis overgrown with some suitable creeper. Walls can also provide an appropriate backcloth for one-sided borders.

The length of the bed makes no difference, but the width should be, if possible, not less than 1 metre (3 ft), so that plants of various sizes can be grown. One-sided borders are not usually wider than 2 metres (6½ ft). The best method is to choose low-growing perennials for the edges and gradually place taller plants further back from the onlooker. Taller perennials should never hide smaller ones.

The method of planting is most important and, before planting, a detailed scheme should be worked out. First, the main requirements for the flowering season must be considered. The border can be in blossom all year round, but if it is preferred to have the bed a mass of colour for one specific period only, this can be ensured by a suitable choice of plants which will flower only at this time. It is easier to select an assortment for a shorter period; simultaneous blooming can be achieved over nearly the whole border much more easily and this always looks very effective. If, on the other hand, the gardener wants to compose a border which will flower all year round, he soon finds out that at least a third of the plants will not flower at a given time.

Therefore, if possible, he should choose such types as are decorative even when they are not flowering, such as grasses and perennials with ornate leaves.

When planting a border, at least three plants of each individual species should be used to make a group, and more than that is even better. The colour composition of those species which flower simultaneously should be borne in mind, otherwise the finest blend of colours may not be obtained. Composite settings can be formed by planting as a spring flowering group, for instance, yellow Leopard's Bane *(Doronicum)*, Bleeding Heart *(Dicentra)* and blue Primrose *(Primula acaulis)*. White *Iberis sempervirens* with yellow Spurge *(Euphorbia polychroma)* and red Tulips provide a beautiful and vivid contrast. Deep blue Delphinium, Oriental Poppy and

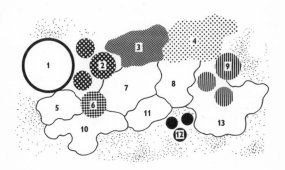

Perennials for moist half-shade
1. *Aruncus silvestris* • 2. *Rodgersia tabularis* • 3. *Thalictrum aquilegifolium* • 4. *Aconitum fischeri* • 5. *Anemone japonica* • 6. *Polygonatum commutatum* • 7. *Astilbe arendsii* • 8. *Hosta sieboldiana* • 9. *Ligularia clivorum* • 10. *Brunnera myosotidiflora* • 11. *Primula denticulata* • 12. *Helleborus niger* • 13. *Ajuga reptans*.

white Ox-eye Daisy are another effective combination for early summer; or scarlet Poppies could be planted in a group with multi-coloured Irises and Lupins, followed by yellow *Eremurus stenophylus* 'Bungei', blue Flax *(Linum perenne)* and coral-red Coral Bells *(Heuchera sanguinea)*. A combination of the Purple Coneflower *(Echinacea purpurea)* with orange *Heliopsis scabra* 'Patula' produces a pleasing effect in summer, while Lavender *(Lavandula officinalis)* with Milfoil *(Achillea tomentosa)*, Coral Bells *(Heuchera)* and Thyme *(Thymus)* make a beautiful combination of low-growing types. Coneflower *(Rudbeckia fulgida* 'Sullivantii') with blue Michaelmas Daisy *(Aster amellus)* in association with a beautiful grass, *Miscanthus sinensis*, is incomparable in late summer. For the same season such low-growing species as Evening Primrose *(Oenothera missouriensis)*, Campion *(Silene schafta)* and *Platycodon grandiflorum* can also be employed. Chrysanthemums and Michaelmas Daisies are particularly representative of autumn, from the low-growing *Aster dumosus* to the tall *Aster novi-belgii*.

Only a few examples of successful flowering combinations have been given, but the possibilities are limitless. It is essential to choose plants which have at least slightly similar requirements as to light and soil conditions.

Well-arranged perennial borders completed, if need be, with some suitable bulbous flowers, especially Tulips, Daffodils and Lilies, and located with an undisturbed secluded background, will become a real source of pleasure and beauty.

A low 'midget' border is a special sort, in which lower-growing species ranging from creeping perennials to perennials up to about 40 cms (16 ins) high are planted. These flower-beds do not need a setting and are located along paths, in front of houses or edging patios and arbours. In this connection full use is made of all sorts of Primulas *(Primula)*, Madwort *(Alyssum montanum* and *A. argenteum)*, Pink *(Dianthus plumarius)*, Lavender *(Lavandula)*, Coral Bells *(Heuchera)*, Catmint *(Nepeta)*, Spurge *(Euphorbia polychroma)*, various

28

Stonecrops *(Sedum)*, Viola *(Viola cornuta)* and Campion *(Silene schafta)*. All types of dwarf bulbous plants flowering in spring and autumn make an excellent supplement. They are particularly suitable as the low-growing, creeping perennials easily cover the empty space left by bulbous flowers when their leaves die away. Paths running alongside these low flower-beds are most beautiful when paved with natural stone.

Perennial edgings, which were so popular at one time, are slowly giving way to other forms in modern gardens, but they do not yet belong entirely to the past. Their main purpose is to separate paths from lawn. It is indisputable that flower edgings along paths are far more pleasant and more suitable than those which are often made from bricks, stone or similar materials.

Early spring and spring perennials
1. *Forsythia suspensa* • 2. *Daphne mezereum* • 3. *Dicentra spectabilis* •
4. *Doronicum columnae* • 5. *Eranthis hiemalis* • 6. *Primula elatior*
'Aurea' • 7. *Helleborus niger* • 8. *Primula acaulis* (blue) • 9. *Primula acaulis* (red) • 10. *Omphalodes verna* • 11. *Primula denticulata* (white).

29

In addition flower edgings can be used round taller flower-beds, where there is no intermediate level before the flat lawn. For instance, rose-beds and formal beds of tall-growing flowers require such a border strip.

A flower border is a very pleasing and welcome embellishment in one further instance. Fruit and vegetable gardens, which are otherwise without decorative features, can be smartened and brightened with a well-kept flower border along the main paths.

The perennials, which are used for edgings, must have certain characteristics in order to fulfil this purpose effectively. They must be dwarf to medium-sized: the most suitable height is up to 40 cms (16 ins). In addition, they must be of compact growth; many creeping perennials, which gradually spread in width through their roots or runners, are less suitable as eventually they choke both the path and the flower-beds which they are supposed to delineate. Finally, they should be decorative even out of the flowering season to look pleasing all year round.

For instance among an appropriate typical assortment are purple-leaved Bugle *(Ajuga)*, yellow Madwort *(Alyssum saxatile* and *A. argenteum)*, dwarf Michaelmas Daisy *(Aster dumosus)*, Megasea *(Bergenia)*, blue *Brunnera myosotidiflora*, grey-leaved Pink *(Dianthus plumarius)*, low-growing and compact Blanket Flower *(Gaillardia hybrida* 'Kobold'), Coral Bells *(Heuchera)*, Plantain Lily *(Hosta)* which is decorative all year round, Lavender *(Lavandula officinalis)*, yellow Flax *(Linum flavum)*, Catmint *(Nepeta mussini)* which flowers for a long time and, after trimming, has a second crop of flower, all sorts of Primulas, Stonecrop *(Sedum spectabile)*, Lamb's Ear *(Stachys lanata)* with its pretty, white felt-like leaves, and various species of Speedwell *(Veronica)* and Catchfly *(Viscaria vulgaris)*.

It is best to compose edgings of just one sort of plant. After several years, when growth needs renewal, this can be replaced with another type of plant so that it does not become boring. Borders made up of several different sorts of plant are never as compact or even. Several different sorts are more often used to edge herbaceous borders or island beds, which are themselves a mixed growth.

Mass groups of perennials bear some relation to herbaceous borders, but with this difference: prolific-flowering varieties alone are mainly used from which larger groups with harmonizing colours are built up. Although individual species in herbaceous borders are planted in threes or in fives at the most, in mass groups they are planted in larger quantities, at least ten to twenty plants in irregular patches.

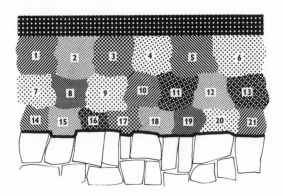

One-sided herbaceous border for summer flowering
1. *Heliopsis scabra* 'Patula' · 2. *Chrysanthemum leucanthemum maximum* · 3. *Helenium hybridum* · 4. *Echinacea purpurea* · 5. *Achillea filipendulina* 'Parker's variety' · 6. *Monarda didyma* · 7. *Aster amellus* · 8. *Gaillardia grandiflora* · 9. *Eremurus stenophylla* 'Bungei' · 10. *Liatris spicata* · 11. *Platycodon grandiflorum* · 12. *Rudbeckia fulgida* 'Sullivantii' · 13. *Astilbe arendsii* · 14. *Oenothera missouriensis* · 15. *Heuchera sanguinea* · 16. *Nepeta mussini* · 17. *Ajuga reptans* · 18. *Viola cornuta* 'Amethyst' · 19. *Stachys lanata* · 20. *Silene schafta* · 21. *Alyssum argenteum*.

31

In contrast to borders or island beds, which are usually located alongside or in the vicinity of paths so that the beauty of individual plants can be closely admired, mass groups are preferably sited in the background, further from public places, but in such a way as to ensure their visibility. These mass groupings should have an appropriate, secluded background, best made up of trees and shrubs and with a peaceful vista provided by a clear uncluttered lawn.

Mass groups of perennials are especially useful in larger, more spacious gardens and parks, with plenty of space and large stretches of lawn, where it is possible to design groups on a grand scale. This can be done even in smaller gardens, but a smaller number of varieties must be chosen and selected very carefully.

Similar principles are involved when drawing up the planting scheme as when designing perennial borders. Here colour combinations are also employed and the principle of correct placing according to the height of the perennials and the stand-point of the observer must be borne in mind.

Of the shorter forms used for borders, the following at least must be mentioned: Madwort *(Alyssum argenteum)*, Michaelmas Daisy *(Aster dumosus)*, Goat's Beard *(Astilbe arendsii)*, Leopard's Bane *(Doronicum)*, Catmint *(Nepeta)* and Stonecrop *(Sedum spectabile)*. Of the taller varieties Italian Starwort and Michaelmas Daisy *(Aster amellus* and *A. novi-belgii)*, Delphinium *(Delphinium)*, *Echinacea*, Orange Sunflower *(Heliopsis)*, *Chrysanthemum morifolium* and Ox-eye Daisy *(Chrysanthemum leucanthemum)*, Russell Lupin, Paeony *(Paeonia albiflora)*, Phlox *(Phlox paniculata)*, Coneflower *(Rudbeckia fulgida speciosa* 'Goldsturm') and Sneezeweed *(Helenium hybridum)* are among the most beautiful.

Modern gardens are noted for freer, irregular shapes, either in the arrangement of deciduous trees and shrubs, conifers, large open expanses of lawn or in flower groups. Similarly perennials, arranged in natural groups, stand out well.

A correct choice of the most suitable types is very important. Those species should be selected and combined which harmonize not only in the colour of their flowers and leaves but in their whole character. Creepers and low-growing perennials, which have a very important function as carpeting plants in natural groupings, are chosen in this way; their attraction lies not only in their flowers but also in their foliage, which, if possible, should be decorative for most of the year. Even plants with insignificant flowers are suitable provided their leaves are evergreen and attractively coloured. For instance, one could choose Bugle *(Ajuga reptans)*,

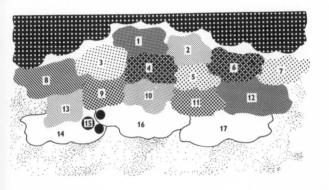

Perennials for grouping in front of shrubs and trees

1. *Rudbeckia nitida* • 2. *Delphinium hybridum* • 3. *Phlox paniculata* (red) • 4. *Phlox paniculata* (pink) • 5. *Chrysanthemum leucanthemum maximum* • 6. *Heliopsis scabra* 'Patula' • 7. *Aruncus silvestris* • 8. *Rudbeckia fulgida* 'Sullivantii' • 9. *Paeonia lactiflora* (pink) • 10. *Doronicum columnae* • 11. *Alyssum argenteum* • 12. Russell Lupin (red) • 13. *Aster novi-belgii* (red) • 14. *Aster dumosus* (white) • 15. *Euphorbia polychroma* • 16. *Oenothera missouriensis* • 17. *Achillea serbica*.

Southernwood *(Artemisia lanata)*, Madwort *(Alyssum montanum)*, dwarf forms of Milfoil *(Achillea)*, Pink *(Dianthus plumarius)*, Perennial Candytuft *(Iberis sempervirens)*, trailing Evening Primrose *(Oenothera missouriensis)*, Rock Soapwort *(Saponaria ocymoides)*, low-growing varieties of Stonecrops *(Sedum)*, Campion *(Silene schafta)*, all species of Thyme *(Thymus)*, all low-growing forms of Speedwell *(Veronica)* and Horned Pansy or Viola *(Viola cornuta)*. Of the grasses, dwarf *Festuca glauca* is very valuable in this context.

First of all a carpet of creeping plants is laid out. Individual species are planted in irregular shapes — some large, some small — to provide a ground-cover of harmonious colours. Then larger and smaller groups of medium-sized and tall perennials are planted in this setting. These groups of perennials should also be carefully selected not only with regard to their flowers but also to their growth and leaves. It is better to choose those varieties which are decorative even after their blooms have faded away.

For example among such low-growing forms are Madwort *(Alyssum argenteum)*, Spiraea or False Goat's Beard *(Astilbe)*, *Brunnera*, *Epimedium*, Spurge *(Euphorbia polychroma)*, Christmas Rose *(Helleborus niger)*, Plantain Lily *(Hosta)*, Lavender *(Lavandula)*, Stonecrop *(Sedum spectabile)* and Sea Lavender *(Statice latifolia)*. Of the grasses, *Avena candida* is indispensable.

From among the taller perennials, the following are very suitable: Bear's Breeches *(Acanthus)*, Windflower *(Anemone vitifolia* var. *robustissima)*, Goat's Beard *(Aruncus)*, Burning Bush *(Dictamnus)*, Foxglove *(Digitalis)*, Echinacea, Day Lily *(Hemerocallis)*, Red Hot Poker *(Kniphofia)* and Mullein *(Verbascum olympicum)*. Among the grasses, all types of *Miscanthus* are appropriate.

Bulbous flowers, arranged in large or small patches, are a very good supplement to natural groupings. The following are all suitable: Daffodil *(Narcissus)*, Star of Bethlehem *(Ornithogallum)*, Crocus, Glory of the Snow *(Chionodoxa)*, Bluebell *(Scilla)*, Grape Hyacinth *(Muscari)*, Snowdrop

*(Galanthus)*, Snowflake *(Leucojum)*, Autumn Crocus *(Colchicum)* and some of the Tulip species *(Tulipa kaufmanniana, T. fosteriana, T. graigii, T. tarda)*. With the exception of some Tulips, all these bulbous plants can be left in the ground for several years without affecting their flowering. They can even be planted among creepers, especially those which do not throw out large roots, for example, Madwort *(Alyssum montanum)*, Milfoil *(Achillea)*, Stonecrop *(Sedum)*, Thyme *(Thymus)* and grasses such as *Festuca*.

Such freely planted groups are often sited near garden

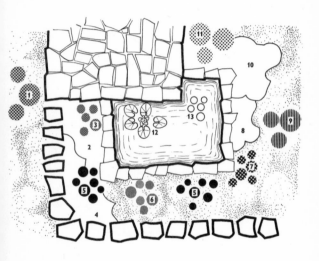

Perennials for planting by water
1. *Helianthus salicifolius* • 2. *Ajuga reptans* • 3. *Hemerocallis fulva* • 4. *Brunnera myosotidiflora* • 5. *Iris germanica* • 6. *Doronicum caucasicum* • 7. *Hosta sieboldiana* • 8. *Tradescantia virginiana* • 9. *Ligularia clivorum* • 10. *Aster novi-belgii* • 11. *Miscanthus sinensis* 'Gigantea' • 12. *Nymphaea hybrida* • 13. *Sagittaria sagittifolia*.

seats and around pools. Bird baths made of natural stone, are an appropriate decorative feature for such areas. So-called 'erratics' can also be placed in the scheme. They are large, isolated boulders of irregular shape, conveniently sunk in the ground and incorporated naturally into the garden to obtain a freer, more 'mountainous' character. The choice of flowers must fit this environment; rock-loving plants would be suitable such as Milfoil *(Achillea serbica)*, Madwort *(Alyssum montanum)*, Sun Rose *(Helianthemum)*, Campion *(Silene schafta)*, Thyme *(Thymus)*, Pheasant's Eye *(Adonis vernalis)*, the Stonecrops *(Sedum)*, and from among the grasses *Festuca* and *Avena* particularly.

Trees and shrubs appropriately sited are also a necessary feature of the modern garden. Of the conifers *Juniperus communis* var. *hibernica*, *Pinus mugo (P. montana)* var. *mughus*, *Pinus silvestris* var. *watereriana*, *Picea glauca* 'Conica', *Picea abies (P. excelsa)* var. *maxwellii* and others are indispensable.

Deciduous shrubs and trees which can be used effectively are *Berberis*, *Betula pendula youngii*, *Cotoneaster praecox*, *Cytisus praecox*, *Daphne mezereum*, *Eleagnus*, *Hippophae*, *Hypericum*, *Potentilla*, *Pyracantha*, *Rosa rugosa*, *Tamarix* and others.

Care should be taken when choosing trees and shrubs, especially when they are for a small garden; in this case it is better to select dwarf varieties which grow slowly.

Planning a garden is an exacting pursuit and without a natural aptitude for this activity it is very difficult to construct a creative lay-out without expert guidance. Several ways of planting are suggested to make this task easier.

Solitaries are usually sizeable plants, either trees, shrubs or flowers, which are conspicuous in themselves and interesting in appearance. They can be both flowering and non-flowering plants. They should be planted singly or in small groups in prominent places in the garden where they form decorative features and talking points, rather in the same way as garden sculpture. Solitary plants can be sited individually either on lawns or near garden seats, terraces, gates or doorways. Perennials with an impressive and ornamental growth are suitable, such as Yarrow *(Achillea filipendulina)*, Sunflower *(Helianthus salicifolius)*, Mullein *(Verbascum olympicum)*, etc.

Striking and distinctive perennials can also be used as 'dot' plants among lower-growing species where their beauty regally asserts itself, especially in naturally planted groups. As examples of appropriate perennials, the following should be mentioned: Bear's Breeches *(Acanthus mollis)*, Southernwood *(Artemisia hybrida)*, Knapweed *(Centaurea macrocephala)*, Delphinium *(Delphinium elatum)*, Burning Bush *(Dictamnus*

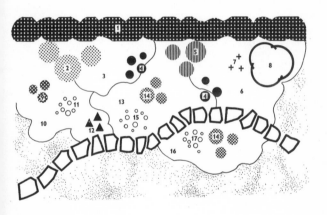

Low-growing perennials which withstand sun and drought

1. Hedge of *Ligustrum ovalifolium* • 2. *Verbascum olympicum* • 3. *Nepeta mussini* • 4. *Alyssum argenteum* • 5. *Echinacea purpurea* • 6. *Alyssum montanum* • 7. *Liatris spicata* • 8. *Cotoneaster praecox* • 9. *Lavandula officinalis* • 10. *Silene schafta* • 11. *Chionodoxa luciliae* • 12. *Sedum spectabile* • 13. *Thymus serpyllum* • 14. *Avena candida* • 15. *Crocus hybridus* • 16. *Sedum spurium* • 17. *Scilla sibirica*.

*albus)*, Foxtail Lily *(Eremurus)*, Day Lily *(Hemerocallis)*, Paeony *(Paeonia)* and, finally, all the tall grasses.

Even a shorter perennial can be a dot plant if it is used for a specific purpose, for instance, a Lavender bush in a patch of Thyme; *Sedum spectabile, Statice latifolia, Tradescantia virginiana, Hosta* and others can be used in the same way.

Flower arrangements are very much a part of the modern interior. Having a garden, it is easy to provide plenty of cut flowers nearly all year round and perennials are one of their main sources. Some species are particularly suitable as cut flowers and last a long time in water.

The gardener is usually reluctant to cut flowers from his formal beds; he prefers them to be admired *in situ*. It is, therefore, better to set up special flower-beds, where flowers are grown solely for cutting. These flower-beds should be sited somewhere apart as the cut stalks are not usually very attractive, but not too far away from the house; it should be possible to fetch flowers at any time, even in bad weather. If there is a piece of ground in the garden reserved for vegetables, usually somewhere behind the house, then this plot is similarly suitable for growing flowers for cutting.

The beds designed for cut flowers should be planted according to the same principles as those for herbaceous borders, that is flowers must be planted according to height.

There are many species which can be used for cutting and it is, therefore, easy to establish a succession of perennials so that flowers are available from early spring almost until November.

Long life is one of our first requirements of cut flowers but this depends not only on the species selected but on what time of day they were picked, and the temperature and humidity of the room in which they are kept. If possible, they should be cut in the morning before the sun has reached them. If they are picked while almost in bud they will generally keep longer than fully opened flowers. The water in the vase should be changed often, and from time to time the ends of the stalks trimmed. Sometimes flowers can be kept fresh a little longer by using one of the various chemicals sold in florists' shops.

Among the most popular varieties with long-lasting flowers are, for instance, Milfoil *(Achillea filipendulina)*, Fleabane *(Erigeron hybridum)*, Chrysanthemum *(Chrysanthemum morifolium)*, Ox-eye Daisy *(Chrysanthemum leucanthemum)*, Pyrethrum *(Chrysanthemum roseum)* as well as Blazing Star *(Liatris spicata)*, Paeony *(Paeonia albiflora)*, Christmas Rose *(Helle-*

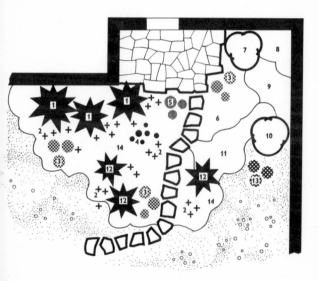

**Perennials for the sunny wild garden**
1. *Pinus mugo* var. *mughus* • 2. *Festuca glauca* • 3. *Avena candida* • 4. *Crocus hybridus* • 5. *Lavandula officinalis* • 6. *Erica carnea* (red) • 7. *Cytisus praecox* • 8. *Aster novi-belgii* (red) • 9. *Aster dumosus* (white) • 10. *Hippophae rhamnoides* • 11. *Erica carnea* (white) • 12. *Juniperus communis* var. *hibernica* • 13. *Eryngium alpinum* • 14. *Thymus serpyllum*.

*borus niger)* and Coneflower *(Rudbeckia nitida)*. In addition, all the above-mentioned types have flowers which do not drop.

Species with their flowers arranged in spikes, such as Delphinium *(Delphinium)*, Russell Lupin, Foxglove *(Digitalis)*, etc., are very decorative in larger vases and, if cut when just beginning to flower, keep for quite a long time, but they have an unpleasant feature in that, while the buds are gradually opening upwards, the bottom flowers die and fall off and make the surroundings untidy.

Some types have flowers which can be dried or which, after fading away, provide attractive seedheads which can be saved for arrangement in dry vases. For instance, Milfoil

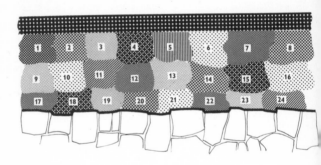

One-sided herbaceous border flowering from spring to autumn
1. Russell Lupin • 2. *Helianthus atrorubens* • 3. *Paeonia albiflora* • 4. *Dephinium hybridum* • 5. *Chrysanthemum leucanthemum maximum* • 6. *Heliopsis scabra* 'Patula' • 7. *Aster novae-angliae* • 8. *Helenium hybridum* • 9. *Chrysanthemum × hortorum* • 10. *Anemone japonica* • 11. *Doronicum columnae* • 12. *Aquilegia hybrida* • 13. *Rudbeckia fulgida* • 14. *Aster novi-belgii* • 15. *Dicentra spectabilis* • 16. *Hemerocallis citrina* • 17. *Primula elatior* 'Aurea' • 18. *Iberis sempervirens* • 19. *Heuchera sanguinea* • 20. *Aster dumosus* • 21. *Bergenia cordifolia* • 22. *Achillea serbica* • 23. *Alyssum argenteum* • 24. *Sedum spectabile*.

*(Achillea filipendulina)*, Globe Thistle *(Echinops ritro)*, Gypsophila), Eulalia *(Miscanthus saccariflorus)*, the stalks and fruits
of Chinese Lantern *(Physalis)*, Sea Lavender *(Statice)*, etc.,
are most suitable for this purpose. The flowers should be cut
just before full bloom and hung somewhere in a dry, dark
room with their blossoms downwards. If the flowers are dried
out in the light, they lose their colour and turn yellow.

A far wider assortment of flowers can be grown for cutting,
of which some are very rewarding. All those suitable are
listed in the summary of perennials according to usage.


# Thinning out perennials

Some perennials multiply very fast by themselves, especially
when they are located in a suitable place, either by seeding
or by spreading roots. These are not good characteristics for
a small garden, where some sorts of perennials must be
thinned out to prevent them spreading more than their
alotted space. It is quite easy with the seeding varieties, if the
faded blossoms are removed in time. An occasional interven-
tion with the hoe can stop the root-spreading species.

This spontaneous propagation, which is a nuisance in small
gardens, is very useful and welcome in larger gardens and
parks, freely and naturally laid out. Here plants are left to
propagate naturally and in so doing larger groups of flowers
are kept beautiful with scarcely any work or effort. The
following are good examples: Madwort *(Alyssum argenteum)*,
Michaelmas Daisy *(Aster amellus)*, *Brunnera myosotidiflora*, Foxglove *(Digitalis gloxiniaeflora)*, Sea Holly *(Eryngium oliveranum)*, Lupin *(Lupinus)*, Evening Primrose *(Oenothera)*,
Golden Rod *(Solidago hybrida)*, Mullein *(Verbascum olympicum)*.

Some perennials are quite a menace because of their

41

spontaneous seeding and care must be taken that their propagation does not become excessive.

The roots of Chinese Lantern *(Physalis franchettii)* are especially invasive and spread very easily if given plenty of moisture and a good soil. Of the grasses, *Miscanthus sacchariflorus* is the most prolific. This characteristic is pleasing enough in larger groupings, but in limited settings it is necessary to take preventive measures. Bearing in mind that the roots do not usually penetrate deep down, they can be obstructed to prevent them spreading in an unwanted direction. Such an obstacle can be formed by a piece of tin or tarred roof covering inserted upright in the ground, about 40—50 cms (16 to 20 ins) deep. It can then be ensured that the roots do not penetrate this obstacle and endanger less aggressive plants in the neighbourhood.

# Suitable combinations of perennials

It has been stressed several times that it is important to the happy development of perennials in the garden to plant compatible species next to each other. A reciprocal ecological relationship is the main criterion: those plants which grow together in their natural environment are nearly always complementary. For example moorland flowers usually grow in impermeable, sandy, non-calcareous soils and consequently usually require these conditions. Other communities are formed by flowers of the steppes, which have had to adapt to specific climatic conditions, characterized by abundant spring rains on which each plant has to exist for the rest of the year, for they are followed by a long period of great heat and drought. There are many tuberous and bulbous plants typical of steppe flora, and these prepare for the dry period by shrivelling up and surviving in a quiescent state. Xerophytic flora is equipped for life in extremely dry places and succulents are typical representatives. Moorland and damp places, in contrast to these dry locations, usually have a sour soil, and similarly there is an entire range of plants which thrive on these conditions. Many plants come from a forest habitat. This is an area in which tall deciduous forests create half-shade and humus, a leafy soil with plenty of moisture. In contrast to this, mountain flora has a completely different environment.

Each of these natural habitats has its own typical flora, which not only thrives well, but also, in effect, blends in appearance. It is necessary to respect these relationships as far as possible in the garden, although the gardener cannot strictly adhere to them because he is growing plants for decoration rather than for the purpose of studying botanical communities. He does not therefore attempt to reproduce these communities exactly and can afford to make various modifications. It is particularly important to see that individual species prosper in given conditions and are mutually complementary in appearance. These are the main criteria to take into consideration when choosing perennials. Naturally the height and colour of the flowers and their flowering season should also be taken into account when preparing the planting schemes.

To make this work easier, a summary of plants which are suitable for mutual combination is provided. This is a sort of brief recipe or guide, which although it cannot fully take the place of the experience and intuitive feeling of a gardener, will be very useful in helping the beginner to avoid basic mistakes.

*Acanthus: Thymus, Festuca, Achillea tomentosa, Adonis, Artemisia lanata, Eryngium alpinum.*
*Aconitum: Anemone japonica, Astilbe, Monarda, Brunnera, Bergenia, Ligularia, Tradescantia.*
*Adonis: Achillea (low), Artemisia lanata, Verbascum olympicum, Avena, Festuca, Lavandula.*

*Achillea filipendulina:* Eryngium, Helenium (red-flowered), *Veronica, Nepeta, Linum perenne.*

*Achillea* (low): Helianthemum, Adonis, Veronica rupestris, *Eryngium, Festuca glauca, Lavandula, Saponaria ocymoides.*

*Ajuga: Anemone japonica, Astilbe, Epimedium, Tradescantia, Trollius.*

*Alyssum:* Achillea, Artemisia, Dianthus, Dictamnus, Eryngium, *Lavandula, Nepeta, Statice latifolia.*

*Anemone japonica:* Aconitum, Chrysanthemum × hortorum, Astilbe (late), Brunnera myosotidiflora, Hosta.

*Aquilegia:* Avena, Campanula persicifolia, Brunnera, Heuchera.

*Artemisia lanata:* Sedum (all), Achillea (low), Adonis, Eryngium *alpinum, Euphorbia polychroma.*

*Artemisia hybrida:* Thymus, Sedum, Alyssum argenteum, Eryngium, *Nepeta, Veronica.*

*Aster amellus:* Avena, Coreopsis, Rudbeckia fulgida, Helenium.

*Aster novae-angliae:* Chrysanthemum × hortorum, Miscanthus, *Aster dumosus, Helianthus.*

*Aster novi-belgii:* Chrysanthemum × hortorum, Rudbeckia fulgida, *Miscanthus, Aster dumosus, Helenium.*

*Aster dumosus:* Avena, Festuca, Aster novi-belgii, Chrysanthemum × hortorum, Anemone japonica.

*Astilbe:* Hosta, Aconitum, Ajuga, Polygonatum, Brunnera, Helleborus, Ligularia, Rodgersia.

*Aruncus:* Astilbe, Digitalis, Bergenia, Hosta, Ligularia.


*Bergenia:* Ajuga, Iris, Doronicum, Brunnera, Euphorbia, Hemerocallis, Avena.

*Brunnera:* Doronicum, Euphorbia polychroma, Tulipa (red and yellow).


*Campanula persicifolia:* Aquilegia, Digitalis, Ajuga, Trollius, *Papaver orientale.*

*Centaurea dealbata:* Scabiosa, Alyssum argenteum, Eremurus, *Avena, Nepeta.*

44

Centaurea macrocephala: Delphinium, Miscanthus, Avena, Statice latifolia, Veronica.

Centaurea montana: Campanula persicifolia, Aquilegia, Papaver orientale, Euphorbia polychroma.

Chrysanthemum × hortorum: Helianthus, Sedum spectabile, Miscanthus, Aconitum, Aster novae-angliae, A. novi-belgii.

Chrysanthemum leucanthemum: Delphinium, Heliopsis, Phlox paniculata, Gypsophila paniculata.

Chrysanthemum roseum: Iris, Papaver orientale, Campanula persicifolia, Aquilegia, Delphinium.

Coreopsis: Platycodon, Nepeta, Delphinium, Echinacea.


Delphinium: Aruncus, Erigeron, Chrysanthemum leucanthemum, Paeonia, Alyssum argenteum, Heliopsis.

Dianthus plumarius: Festuca, Avena, Veronica, Alyssum argenteum, Achillea (low), Eryngium, Euphorbia, Lavandula, Platycodon, Thymus.

Dicentra: Doronicum, Primula, Brunnera, Tulipa species, Narcissus.

Dictamnus: Festuca, Avena, Achillea (low), Alyssum argenteum, Lavandula, Linum flavum, Oenothera missouriensis.

Digitalis: Campanula persicifolia, Verbascum olympicum, Avena, Festuca, Brunnera, Geum, Veronica.

Doronicum: Brunnera, Bergenia, Dicentra, Primula acaulis, Tulipa species, Omphalodes.


Echinacea: Heliopsis, Coreopsis, Statice latifolia, Stachys lanata, Achillea (low), Miscanthus, Avena.

Echinops: Dictamnus, Gypsophila paniculata, Heliopsis, Solidago.

Epimedium: Primula, Omphalodes, Ajuga, Hepatica, small bulbous plants.

Eremurus: Alyssum argenteum, Heuchera, Linum perenne, Avena, Festuca.

Erigeron: Artemisia, Chrysanthemum leucanthemum, Oenothera missouriensis, Helenium.

45

*Eryngium:* Gypsophila repens, Heuchera, Geum, Thymus, Achillea (low), Lavandula, Festuca, Avena.
*Euphorbia polychroma:* Brunnera, Tulipa, Muscari, Iberis, Thymus, Festuca.

*Gaillardia:* Chrysanthemum roseum, Chrysanthemum leucanthemum, Heliopsis, Delphinium, Oenothera missouriensis.
*Geum:* Doronicum, Brunnera, Veronica, Euphorbia polychroma, Viola cornuta, Iberis.
*Gypsophila:* Chrysanthemum leucanthemum, Echinacea, Heliopsis.

*Helleborus:* Brunnera, Omphalodes, Primula acaulis, P. denticulata, P. rosea, Polygonatum, Epimedium.
*Helenium:* Papaver orientale, Centaurea montana, Physostegia, Phlox paniculata, Nepeta, Echinacea, Miscanthus.
*Helianthemum:* Veronica, Linum perenne, Thymus, Festuca, Avena, Artemisia lanata, Achillea tomentosa.
*Helianthus:* Aster novi-belgii, A. novae-angliae, A. amellus, Miscanthus, Chrysanthemum × hortorum.
*Heliopsis:* Delphinium, Chrysanthemum leucanthemum, Echinacea, Phlox paniculata, Veronica, Nepeta.
*Hemerocallis:* Hosta, Tradescantia, Delphinium, Iris, Ligularia, Miscanthus, Avena, Papaver orientale.
*Heuchera:* Viola cornuta, Nepeta, Oenothera, Veronica, Ajuga, Linum perenne.
*Hosta:* Astilbe, Ajuga, Brunnera, Monarda, Polygonatum, Rodgersia.

*Iberis:* Geum, Phlox subulata, Euphorbia polychroma, Alyssum montanum, Primula elatior, Trollius.
*Incarvillea:* Viola cornuta, Avena, Brunnera, Euphorbia polychroma, Linum flavum.
*Iris germanica:* Papaver orientale, Lupinus, Heuchera, Avena, Veronica, Viscaria.

46

*Kniphofia:* Yucca, Avena, Miscanthus, Aster amellus, Platycodon, Chrysanthemum × hortorum.

*Lavandula:* Achillea tomentosa, Artemisia lanata, Oenothera, Festuca, Helianthemum, Thymus, Heuchera, Sedum.
*Liatris:* Statice latifolia, Platycodon, Linum perenne, Coreopsis verticillata.
*Ligularia:* Aconitum, Miscanthus, Astilbe, Hosta, Rodgersia.
*Linum flavum:* Dictamnus, Eryngium, Heuchera, Scabiosa.
*Linum perenne:* Alyssum argenteum, Heuchera, Coreopsis verticillata.
*Lupinus:* Thalictrum, Hemerocallis, Papaver orientale, Delphinium.
*Lychnis chalcedonica:* Chrysanthemum leucanthemum, Delphinium.

*Macleaya:* Avena, Hosta, Oenothera, Statice latifolia.
*Miscanthus:* Kniphofia, Hosta, Aster amellus, Rudbeckia fulgida.
*Monarda:* Astilbe, Aconitum, Miscanthus, Hosta, Tradescantia.

*Nepeta:* Alyssum argenteum, Viscaria, Coreopsis verticillata, Rudbeckia fulgida, Helenium, Oenothera, Heuchera.

*Oenothera missouriensis:* Nepeta, Veronica, Viola cornuta, Campanula persicifolia, Avena candida.
*Omphalodes verna:* Dicentra, Primula, Epimedium, Doronicum.

*Paeonia:* Iris, Lupinus, Hemerocallis, Chrysanthemum leucanthemum, Delphinium.
*Papaver orientale:* Lupinus, Iris, Delphinium, Aruncus, Alyssum argenteum.
*Phlox paniculata:* Rudbeckia, Gypsophila paniculata, Helenium, Aster amellus, Monarda, Solidago.
*Physalis:* Sedum, Aster dumosus, Festuca, Avena, Silene schafta.
*Physostegia:* Aconitum, Viola cornuta, Aster amellus, A. dumosus, Festuca, Avena, Achillea serbica.
*Platycodon:* Liatris, Aster amellus, Veronica, Artemisia, Oenothera, Silene schafta, Avena candida.

47

*Polygonatum:* Aconitum, Anemone japonica, Astilbe, Aruncus, Brunnera, Epimedium, Helleborus, Ligularia, Primula.

*Primula:* all other *Primula* types, Bergenia, Brunnera, Doronicum, Epimedium, Omphalodes, Trollius.

*Rodgersia:* Aconitum, Astilbe, Aruncus, Brunnera, Hosta, Ligularia, Omphalodes, Polygonatum, Tradescantia.

*Rudbeckia fulgida:* Aster amellus, Echinacea, Helenium, Platycodon, Phlox paniculata, Miscanthus, Avena.

*Rudbeckia nitida:* Miscanthus, Aster amellus, Solidago, Phlox paniculata, Physostegia, Monarda, Helenium.

*Saponaria ocymoides:* Veronica, Achillea serbica, Viscaria, Avena, Festuca.

*Scabiosa:* Rudbeckia fulgida, Oenothera missouriensis, Avena, Veronica.

*Sedum:* other types, Adonis, Achillea, Alyssum, Artemisia, Dianthus, Eryngium, Helianthemum, Lavandula, Nepeta, Silene schafta, Statice, Thymus, Verbascum.

*Silene schafta:* Sedum, Platycodon, Avena, Festuca, Eryngium, Kniphofia, Linum perenne, Nepeta.

*Solidago:* Aster novi-belgii, A. novae-angliae, A. amellus, Chrysanthemum × hortorum, Helenium, Phlox paniculata, Miscanthus, Physostegia.

*Stachys grandiflora:* Hosta, Avena, Silene schafta, Achillea filipendulina, Liatris, Platycodon.

*Stachys lanata:* Veronica, Dianthus, Ajuga, Alyssum argenteum, Avena, Euphorbia, Heuchera, Platycodon.

*Statice latifolia:* Silene schafta, Thymus, Achillea, Coreopsis verticillata, Echinacea, Helenium, Avena, Oenothera, Liatris, Rudbeckia fulgida.

*Thalictrum:* Delphinium, Hemerocallis, Aquilegia, Trollius, Brunnera, Epimedium.

48

*Thymus:* Sedum, Achillea, Dianthus, Eryngium, Avena, Festuca, Alyssum, Artemisia, Aster dumosus, Helianthemum.
*Tradescantia:* Iris, Hemerocallis, Trollius, Hosta, Bergenia, Viola.
*Trollius:* Thalictrum, Tradescantia, Iris, Hemerocallis, Bergenia, Ajuga, Brunnera.

*Verbascum:* Veronica, Avena, Alyssum, Eryngium, Sedum, Nepeta.
*Veronica:* Coreopsis verticillata, Thymus, Festuca, Avena, Viscaria, Scabiosa, Sedum, Heuchera, Linum flavum.
*Viola cornuta:* Iberis, Geum, Tulipa, Oenothera, Alyssum argenteum, Stachys lanata, Bergenia, Avena, Euphorbia polychroma.
*Viscaria:* Dianthus plumarius, Nepeta, Veronica, Cerastium, Aster alpinus.

# Table showing the requirements and usage of perennial

Explanatory notes: *sun* ○  *half-shade* ●  *dry soil* 1  *medium soil* 2
*damp soil* 3  *solitary* ×  *herbaceous border* ∞  *natural group* ∴.
*rockery* □  *edging* =  *cut flower* ∧  *carpeting plant* ∞,
in winter dryness w. d., winter shelter w. s., for covering pergolas and fences *)

| *Species* | *Soil* | *Position* | *Use* | *Note* |
|---|---|---|---|---|
| *Acanthus mollis* | 2 | ○ | × ∴. | *w. d.* |
| *Achillea filipendulina* | 1 2 | ○ | × ∞ ∴. | |
| *Achillea serbica* | 1 | ○ | ∴. □ = ∞ | |
| *Achillea tomentosa* | 1 | ○ | ∴. □ = ∞ | |
| *Aconitum fischeri* | 2 3 | ○ ● | ∞ ∴. ∧ | |
| *Aconitum napellus* | 3 | ● | ∞ ∴. ∧ | |
| *Adonis amurensis* | 1 2 | ○ | ∴. □ | |
| *Adonis vernalis* | 1 | ○ | ∴. □ | |
| *Ajuga reptans* | 2 3 | ○ ● | ∴. □ = ∞ | |
| *Alyssum argenteum* | 1 2 | ○ | ∞ ∴. | |
| *Alyssum saxatile* | 1 | ○ | ∴. □ = ∞ | |
| *Anemone japonica* | 3 | ● | ∞ ∴. ∧ | |
| *Aquilegia hybrida* | 2 | ○ ● | ∞ ∴. ∧ | |
| *Artemisia hybrida* | 1 | ○ | × ∴. | |
| *Artemisia lanata* | 1 | ○ | ∴. □ ∞ | |
| *Aruncus silvester* | 2 | ● | × ∴. ∧ | |
| *Aster amellus* | 1 2 | ○ ● | ∞ ∴. ∧ | |
| *Aster dumosus* | 2 | ○ | ∞ ∴. □ = | |
| *Aster novae-angliae* | 2 | ○ | ∞ ∴. ∧ | |
| *Aster novi-belgii* | 2 | ○ | ∞ ∴. ∧ | |
| *Astilbe arendsii* | 2 3 | ● | ∞ ∴. ∧ | |

| Species | Soil | Position | Use | Note |
|---|---|---|---|---|
| Bergenia cordifolia | 2 3 | ○ ● | ∞ ∴ □ | |
| Brunnera myosotidiflora | 2 3 | ○ ● | ∞ ∴ □ | |
| Campanula persicifolia | 2 | ○ | ∞ ∴ ∧ | |
| Centaurea dealbata | 1 2 | ○ | ∞ ∴ ∧ | |
| Centaurea macrocephala | 1 | ○ | × ∴ ∧ | |
| Centaurea montana | 2 3 | ○ | ∞ ∴ ∧ | |
| Chrysanthemum × hortorum | 2 | ○ | ∞ ∴ ∧ | |
| Chrysanthemum maximum | 2 | ○ | ∞ ∧ | |
| Chrysanthemum roseum | 2 | ○ | ∞ ∧ | |
| Coreopsis grandiflora | 2 | ○ | ∞ ∧ | |
| Coreopsis verticillata | 2 | ○ | ∞ ∴ | |
| Delphinium cultorum | 2 | ○ | × ∞ ∴ ∧ | |
| Dianthus plumarius | 1 | ○ | ∞ ∴ □ = ∧ ∼ | |
| Dicentra spectabilis | 2 | ○ ● | ∞ ∴ | |
| Dictamnus albus | 1 | ○ | × ∴ | |
| Digitalis purpurea 'Gloxiniaeflora' | 2 | ○ | ∞ ∴ ∧ | |
| Doronicum caucasicum | 2 3 | ○ ● | ∞ ∴ ∧ | |
| Doronicum columnae | 2 3 | ○ ● | ∞ ∴ ∧ | |
| Echinacea purpurea | 1 2 | ○ | ∞ ∴ ∧ | |
| Echinops ritro | 1 | ○ | ∞ ∴ ∧ | |
| Epimedium spp. | 2 3 | ● | ∴ □ | |
| Eremurus spp. | 2 | ○ | × ∴ ∧ | w. d., w. s. |
| Erigeron hybridus | 2 | ○ | ∞ ∴ ∧ | |
| Eryngium alpinum | 1 | ○ | ∴ ∧ | |
| Eryngium bourgatii | 1 | ○ | ∴ □ | |
| Eryngium oliveranum | 1 | ○ | ∞ ∴ ∧ | |
| Euphorbia polychroma | 2 | ○ | ∞ ∴ □ = | |
| Gaillardia hybrida | 1 | ○ | ∞ ∧ | w. d. |
| Geum chiloense | 2 | ○ | ∞ ∴ | |
| Geum hybridum | 2 | ○ | ∞ ∴ | |
| Gypsophila paniculata | 1 2 | ○ | ∴ ∧ | |
| Helenium hybridum | 2 | ○ | ∞ ∴ ∧ | |
| Helianthemum hybridum | 1 | ○ | ∴ □ = | |
| Helianthus spp. | 2 | ○ | ∞ ∴ ∧ | |
| Helianthus salicifolius | 2 | ○ | × ∴ | |
| Heliopsis scabra | 2 | ○ | ∞ ∴ ∧ | |
| Helleborus spp. | 2 3 | ● | ∞ ∴ □ ∧ | |

51

| Species | Soil | Position | Use | Note |
|---|---|---|---|---|
| Hemerocallis spp. | 2 | ○ ● | × ∞ ∴ ∧ | |
| Heuchera sanguinea | 2 3 | ○ ● | ∞ ∴ □ = ∧ | |
| Hosta spp. | 2 3 | ○ ● | ∞ ∴ = | |
| Iberis sempervirens | 1 2 | ○ | ∴ □ = ∿ | |
| Incarvillea delavayi | 2 | ○ | ∞ ∴ | w. d., w. s. |
| Incarvillea grandiflora | 2 | ○ | ∴ □ | w. d., w. s. |
| Iris germanica | 2 | ○ ● | ∞ ∴ ∧ | |
| Kniphofia hybrida | 2 | ○ | ∞ ∴ ∧ | w. s. |
| Lathyrus latifolius | 1 2 | ○ | ∧ | *) |
| Lavandula officinalis | 1 | ○ | ∞ ∴ = | |
| Liatris spicata | 1 2 | ○ | ∞ ∴ ∧ | |
| Ligularia spp. | 3 | ○ ● | × ∴ | |
| Linum flavum var. compactum | 2 | ○ ● | ∞ ∴ □ | |
| Linum perenne | 1 2 | ○ | ∞ ∴ | |
| Lupinus polyphyllus | 2 | ○ ● | ∞ ∴ ∧ | |
| Lychnis chalcedonica | 2 | ○ ● | ∞ ∴ | |
| Macleaya cordata | 2 | ○ ● | × ∴ | |
| Miscanthus spp. | 2 | ○ ● | × ∴ ∧ | w. d., w. s. |
| Monarda didyma | 2 | ○ ● | ∞ ∴ ∧ | |
| Nepeta spp. | 1 | ○ | ∞ ∴ □ = | |
| Oenothera missouriensis | 1 2 | ○ | ∞ ∴ □ = ∿ | |
| Omphalodes verna | 2 3 | ● | ∴ □ = | |
| Paeonia lactiflora | 2 | ○ | × ∞ ∧ | |
| Papaver orientalis | 2 | ○ | ∞ ∴ | |
| Phlox paniculata | 2 | ○ | ∞ ∴ ∧ | |
| Physalis spp. | 2 3 | ○ ● | ∞ ∧ | |
| Physostegia virginiana | 2 | ○ ● | ∞ ∴ ∧ | |
| Platycodon grandiflorum | 2 | ○ ● | ∞ ∴ □ ∧ | |
| Polygonatum spp. | 2 3 | ● | ∴ | |
| Primula denticulata | 2 3 | ○ ● | ∞ ∴ □ = | |
| Primula elatior | 2 | ○ ● | ∞ ∴ □ = ∧ | |
| Primula rosea | 3 | ○ ● | ∞ ∴ □ = | |
| Primula vulgaris | 2 3 | ● | ∞ ∴ □ = | |
| Rodgersia spp. | 3 | ● | × ∴ | |
| Rudbeckia fulgida | 2 | ○ | ∞ ∴ ∧ | |
| Rudbeckia nitida | 2 | ○ | ∴ ∧ | |
| Saponaria ocymoides | 1 | ○ | ∴ □ = | |

| Species | Soil | Position | Use | Note |
|---|---|---|---|---|
| *Scabiosa caucasica* | 1 2 | ○ | $\infty \therefore \wedge$ | |
| *Sedum spectabile* | 1 2 | ○ | $\infty \therefore \square =$ | |
| *Sedum* (low species) | 1 | ○ | $\therefore \square = \infty$ | |
| *Silene schafta* | 1 | ○ | $\therefore \square = \infty$ | |
| *Solidago hybrida* | 2 | ○ | $\infty \therefore \wedge$ | |
| *Stachys* spp. | 1 | ○ | $\infty \therefore \square = \infty$ | |
| *Statice latifolia* | 1 | ○ | $\infty \therefore \wedge$ | |
| *Thalictrum* spp. | 2 3 | ○ ● | $\infty \therefore \wedge$ | |
| *Thymus serpyllum* | 1 | ○ | $\therefore \square \infty$ | |
| *Tradescantia virginiana* | 2 3 | ○ ● | $\infty \therefore$ | |
| *Trollius hybridus* | 2 3 | ○ | $\infty \therefore \wedge$ | |
| *Verbascum olympicum* | 1 | ○ | $\times \therefore$ | |
| *Veronica* spp. | 1 2 | ○ | $\infty \therefore \square =$ | |
| *Viola cornuta* | 2 3 | ○ | $\therefore \square = \infty$ | |
| *Viscaria vulgaris* | 2 | ○ | $\infty \therefore = \wedge$ | |

# PLATES

*Individual types are arranged and graded in order of flowering from early spring to late autumn.*
*The average height of each plant is given in centimetres; the conversion to feet and inches is approximate only.*
*Roman numerals indicate the month when the plant flowers.*

## MONTHS AND SEASONS

The months and seasons mentioned in this book apply to temperate regions of the northern hemisphere (Europe, Canada and the northern United States). For readers living in other regions, the following table gives approximate equivalents.

Subtropical regions of the northern hemisphere
*(Mediterranean sea, southern United States)*

Plants will tend to shoot and flower a month or so earlier in these regions.

Tropical regions *(around the Equator)*

No seasons exist in the tropical regions. There are no set times for planting, and the suitability of growing an individual plant will depend on local climatic conditions.

Subtropical regions of the southern hemisphere
*(Australasia, South America, southern Africa)*

The seasons are reversed in these regions. Spring is approximately from September to November, summer from December to February, autumn from March to May, and winter from June to August.

## *Helleborus*

HELLEBORE

20—40 cms (8—16 ins); II—III

Ranunculaceae

The Buttercup Family

The Hellebores, because of their beauty and many advantages, are a valuable inclusion in any garden. Their large anemone-like blossoms open early in the spring, often even during winter and in some species as early as autumn. They have deep green, palmate leaves of a leathery texture.

*Helleborus niger*, the Christmas Rose, is the most beautiful variety, flowering from February to March with pure white blossoms. *H. niger* var. *praecox* is also an early flowering form; it is often in flower as early as November onwards.

All Hellebores love a good, deep, mildly calcareous soil with adequate moisture and half-shade. The plants can be kept for many years without being lifted and will still flower beautifully. They respond very well to an occasional mulching with a good compost.

Under the group name *H. orientalis* various forms of Hellebore are grown which have white, pink and purple blossoms. They are tall (up to 40 cms; 16 ins) and flower in spring, usually in March.

All Hellebores are suitable for combining with groups of early spring flowers such as Primroses and many of the bulbous plants which grow well in half-shade and require similar soil.

The easiest method of propagation is by division, and this is best done at the end of summer. It is possible to grow some varieties from seed *(H. niger, H. orientalis)*, but the plants produced may differ from the parent plants. The seed should be sown immediately after it ripens. The plants begin to flower in the third year after being sown. They should be planted at intervals of 30—40 cms (12—16 ins).

*Helleborus niger*

# *Adonis*

PHEASANT'S EYE

20—30 cms (8—12 ins); II—V

Ranunculaceae

The Buttercup Family

Pheasant's Eyes are among the first messengers of spring, and their large yellow blossoms please every nature-lover. Two species are mainly cultivated in gardens: the very early *Adonis amurensis* and *A. vernalis* which flowers later.

*A. amurensis*, which originally came from Manchuria, is about 20—25 cms (8—9½ ins) high in the flowering season. It is very early and one of the first flowers in the garden. If the winter is a mild one, it flowers as early as February and its blossoms last until March. The golden-yellow, buttercup-like flowers are quite large, with a silky sheen on the petals. The leaves start forming only when the flowers are fading. They are finely divided and look rather like ferns. At the end of May and in June the leaves turn yellow and dry up and the plant dies away.

*A. amurensis* is very hardy; it needs scarcely any care and flowers every year. Its only requirements are a light soil and full sun, but it should be protected against excessive winter dampness.

It can be used in spring flower-beds together with Pasque Flowers, early Crocuses, etc. It is often grown in rockeries also

It can only be propagated by division; the best time to do this is in late spring when the leaves die away. It is not grown from seed

The flowers of *A. vernalis* are very similar to *A. amurensis*, but appear later, from March to May, and the leaves are more slenderly divided. It requires the same conditions as *A. amurensis*, but can be propagated from seed as well as by division; it can also be used in the same way.

*Adonis vernalis*

# *Primula denticulata*

Primulaceae
The Primrose Family

20—30 cms (8—12 ins); IV

The Primrose family covers an immense range and diversity of species and varieties. It is divided into several groups according to appearance and particularly the arrangement of flowers within the inflorescence.

*Primula denticulata* belongs to the groups with globular flower-heads. It comes from the mountains of Asia, but has been cultivated in European gardens for a very long time. The inflorescence, made up of many small flowers, forms a ball at the top of a stalk 20—30 cms (8—12 ins) high. The basic type has flowers of a light lilac-blue colour, but other colours have been developed, such as white, deep violet, and all shades of pink to carmine-red. The leaves are lance-shaped and form a basal rosette, which grows more thickly after flowering. It flowers with the first Primroses in April.

It is hardy, and grows well in the average garden soil provided this is not too dry, either in half-shade or in full sun.

It is used in mixed groups of spring flowers in the same way as *P. acaulis* and *P. elatior* (see later). Spring is the best time for propagation, either by division or, even more successful, by sowing the very fine seed directly after it has been gathered.

*P. rosea*, which comes from the damp meadows of the Himalayas, also belongs to this group. It is smaller, only 10—15 cms (4—6 ins) high and also flowers in April. The vivid pink flowers are larger and arranged in spires rather than in a regular ball as the former variety. It is very beautiful and flowers freely, if provided with a suitable position (damp, marsh-like soil either in half-shade or sun).

It is very appropriate for the banks of streams or pools and for artificial and natural moorland. It is propagated from seed and by division, and is even self-seeding in suitable conditions. It should be planted at intervals of 20—30 cms (8—12 ins).

*Primula denticulata*

# *Primula acaulis*

Primulaceae
The Primrose Family

15—30 cms (6—12 ins); IV—V

*Primula acaulis* belongs to the group of Primroses which form neat, compact, cushion-like growth. Its flowers are borne individually on short stalks, straight out of the leaf rosette. In full bloom they form cushions 10—15 cms (4—6 ins) high. It is one of the first to flower, from as early as the beginning of April until May. The blossoms usually have yellow 'eyes' on a white, blue, pink, red or yellow ground. They grow best in a moist soil with plenty of humus and in partial shade. They are propagated mainly by seed, though it is also possible to divide them.

*P. elatior*, Oxlip, is another, very pleasing variety. Its flowers are very similar to *P. acaulis*, but they are arranged in a different way. They have a 'candelabra' form of flower with one main stem branching at the top into an umbel in which each floret is set individually. The flowering plant forms quite large clumps up to 30 cms (12 ins) high. It flowers a little later than *P. acaulis* with yellow, red, white and pink to violet blossoms. A clear blue colour is uncommon. It grows in the same conditions as *P. acaulis* but it will tolerate more sunshine.

Both Primulas are suitable for mixed planting with spring flowers. They come in a rich range of colours, which enables the gardener to obtain a beautiful and vivid display, particularly with the addition of bulbous plants. They are effectively propagated from seed in spring, best of all in a cold-frame. In summer the young plants are ready to be put out and they flower as early as the following spring. They should be planted 30 cms (12 ins) apart.

*Primula acaulis*

# *Bergenia cordifolia*

MEGASEA

30—40 cms (12—16 ins); IV—V

Saxifragaceae
The Saxifrage Family

Megaseas are very hardy and tenacious perennials native to Siberia and the Altai. They form strong roots from which grow large, evergreen, glossy leaves which in some varieties turn a beautiful red in autumn. The pink or pinky-red flowers, which appear in March or April, are arranged in clusters on stout, leafless stalks up to 40 cms (16 ins) high.

*Bergenia cordifolia* has dark green, heart-shaped leaves and its flowers are pinky-red. It is 40 cms (16 ins) high. The leaves of the slightly shorter *B. hybrida* 'Evening Glow' turn an attractive bronze shade in autumn, and it has purple-red flowers. *B. hybrida* 'Silver Light' is a lovely vigorous white variety, pink-flushed in bud and growing to about 40 cms (16 ins) in height.

The plants thrive best in partial shade, but they can even stand full shade or sunshine. They need a nourishing soil, with adequate moisture, but they can survive in dry conditions.

It is possible to plant them in rockeries as solitaries; they also stand out well near stretches of water or in group plantings with creepers, grasses and ferns. They are ornamental even when not in flower because of their handsome, evergreen foliage.

Megaseas can remain for a very long time in one place without being transplanted and cared for. They can be propagated from seed, but in the first instance it is better to split them or take cuttings in autumn or early spring.

*Bergenia cordifolia*

# *Doronicum*

LEOPARD'S BANE

30—50 cms (12—20 ins); IV—V

Compositae

The Daisy Family

This well-known and popular spring perennial, with golden-yellow flowers similar to Ox-eye Daisies, brings one of the earliest splashes of colour to the garden. Two types are most commonly planted. The first, *Doronicum caucasicum*, is the earlier and smaller, 30—40 cms (12—16 ins) high; it flowers in the second half of March and in April. It comes from the Caucasus and the mountains of Asia Minor. The flowers are 4—5 cms (1½—2 ins) in diameter and grow in groups of two or three on a stalk. The second, *D. plantagineum*, is similar but it is a little taller, 40—50 cms (16—20 ins), and the flowers are nearly double in size. It has long, narrow leaves, and flowers at the beginning of May. The variety 'Harpur Crew' is recommended for its large flowers and branching stems.

Leopard's Bane is very popular and deservedly so, for it has a wide range of uses in the garden. The shorter *D. caucasicum* is suitable for rockeries and both species are suitable for informal arrangements of early spring flowers combined with, for instance, Primulas, Tulips and other bulbs which flower at that time and harmonize in colour with them. They are also suitable for cutting, though the flowers are not especially long-lived.

The plants are very easy and trouble-free and will grow in almost every garden soil, as long as it is not allowed to become too dry in summer. They prefer partial shade with adequate moisture.

They are easily propagated by division directly after the flowers fade. The plants can remain in one place for several years without special care, but it is a good idea to divide and transplant them after four or five years and so rejuvenate them. Leopard's Banes should be planted at intervals of 40 cms (16 ins).

*Doronicum caucasicum*

66

# *Epimedium*

20—30 cms (8—12 ins); IV—V

*Epimedium* is an attractive spring flower, for not only are its delicate sprays of pendent, four-petalled blossoms picturesque but its leaves, which last all year, are very decorative. The foliage of many varieties changes colour at the end of summer and in autumn or is bronze- or purple-tinted when young. Epimediums were first cultivated in Europe and Asia. They are usually quite similar to one another, and their chief difference is in the colour of their flowers. One of the most attractive is *Epimedium alpinum* 'Rubrum', with heart-shaped, red-veined leaves grouped in threes. In autumn the leaves turn a beautiful red and last throughout winter. The flowers are attractive; the outer sepals are red, while the inner petals are white. *E. a.* 'Lilacinum' is lilac-blue. They are both very decorative and last a long time in one place. *E. pinnatum* 'Colchicum' is like the former, but with yellow flowers and beautifully green leaves which do not change colour in autumn. It requires a warmer situation. *E. youngianum* 'Niveum' is slightly smaller, 15—25 cms (6—10 ins) and the flowers are larger and pure white.

All thrive well in an average garden soil with sufficient moisture; they are long-lived and do not require any special care. Although naturally shade-loving woodland plants, they are adaptable to any but hot dry positions. In half-shade under thick trees, they form beautiful, weed-free, dense clumps.

They are propagated most easily by splitting up old plants or by root cuttings in autumn. It is also possible to propagate the species from seed. They should be planted at intervals of 30 cms (12 ins).

*Epimedium alpinum* 'Rubrum'

# *Iberis sempervirens*                              Cruciferae

## PERENNIAL CANDYTUFT   The Wallflower Family
15—25 cms (6—10 ins); IV—V

Candytufts are very valuable, small, cushion-forming perennials
which as a result of their modest requirements, ease of cultivation
and beauty play a varied role in the garden.

*Iberis sempervirens*, which comes from southern Europe, is the
variety most commonly planted. It forms dense, cushion-like tufts
with narrow, dark green leaves which last through winter. The
plant is covered in the flowering season with snow-white flowers
which are grouped in dense, flat racemes at the top of the stalks.
Numerous varieties of Perennial Candytuft have been developed.

*Iberis sempervirens* 'Findel' is a strong-growing variety with large
flowers, about 20 cms (8 ins) high; *I. s.* 'Snowflake', up to 25 cms
(10 ins) high, is large-flowered; *I. s.* 'Little Gem' is only about
15 cms (6 ins) high and is a little weaker in growth.

Candytufts should be planted in a good, deep, humous soil
which is not too damp. The location should be a sunny one; it can
stand mild half-shade, but the bushes are then not as compact and
low-growing.

Candytuft is indispensable in the rockery and on garden walls
where it forms waterfalls and cascades of white blossom. It is
excellently suited for borders where it can be combined with red
Tulips and other colourful flowers.

After the flowers fade away, it is a good idea to trim the plant by
about a third, to encourage it to get thicker, and to add a good
feed. It will then last in one place for many years.

It is propagated by cuttings in August. It should be planted out
at intervals of 30—40 cms (12—16 ins).

*Iberis sempervirens* 'Snowflake'

70

# *Omphalodes*
### BLUE-EYED MARY
10—15 cms (4—6 ins); IV—V

Boraginaceae
The Borage Family

This is an attractive, small spring flower with blue flowers reminiscent of Forget-me-nots.

*Omphalodes verna* is the best known, originating in southern Europe, where it grows in the forests of limestone regions. That is why it grows best in mild half-shade, in reasonably moist humous soil. If suitable conditions are provided, it forms wild clumps often spreading to a considerable width. It contrasts well with various types of Primulas, Hellebores, Leopard's Bane and other spring flowers. Apart from the blue variety, there is also a beautiful white form, *O. verna* var. *alba*.

*Omphalodes* shows to great advantage in a slightly overshadowed rockery, or as a spring planting under thinly planted trees. It is a very rewarding and agreeable flower, which should not be absent from any garden.

It is propagated easily by division or by stem and root cuttings. It is advisable to plant young seedlings in flower-pots, and to leave intervals of 15 cms (6 ins) when later planting them out in the garden. When propagated in spring, the plants are ready to be transplanted in autumn.

*Omphalodes verna*

## *Alyssum*
MADWORT
5—50 cms (2—20 ins); IV—VII

Cruciferae
The Wallflower Family

Perennial species of this family are mostly of a low-growing and creeping habit and usually have white flowers. Their home is the Mediterranean and Central Europe. They are fastidious and sun-loving. Three types are especially important for gardens. The first is *Alyssum argenteum*, 40—50 cms (16—20 ins) tall [VI—VII], which forms compact bushes with narrow grey leaves. Its minute golden-yellow flowers are arranged in flat racemes at the top of the stalks. The soil should be light, well drained and rather dry. This plant withstands considerable dryness very well. It should be planted at intervals of 35 cms (14 ins). It is suitable for larger rockeries or formal flower-beds and even for informal groups, where it shows up well against a carpet of low-growing flowers. It is propagated very easily by seed and division.

*A. montanum*, 5—15 cms (2—6 ins) tall [IV—V], is a low-growing creeper, forming cushions of round silvery-grey leaves. Small golden-yellow flowers cover the whole plant in the flowering season. In spring it is invaluable as a creeper for rockeries, dry walls, borders and as a carpeting plant in informal groups. It needs a permeable, well-drained rather poor, calcareous soil. It is propagated very well by seed, or even by cuttings. It should be planted at intervals of 30 cms (12 ins).

*A. saxatile*, 20—25 cms (8—10 ins) tall [IV—V] forms compact shrubs with grey-green leaves and thick-branched racemes of golden-yellow flowers. It grows very well in a sunny place in a dry, calcareous soil. It is suitable for rockeries and borders. It is propagated from seed, and should be planted at intervals of 30 cms (12 ins).

*Alyssum saxatile*

74

## *Dicentra*

BLEEDING HEART

40—60 cms (1¼—2 ft); V

Papaveraceae

The Poppy Family

Bleeding Heart is a perennial of a unique appearance and beauty. The flowers and their structure are most interesting: each forms a stylized multi-coloured heart.

*Dicentra spectabilis*, originating in Japan, is of the many species known the most beautiful and most frequently cultivated type in gardens. It has fleshy fragile roots and forms shrubby plants with fleshy stalks, terminating in thin clusters of flowers. The flowers are suspended from arching stems. They are very pretty, with pinky-red exterior sepals, forming a typical heart-shape and with white interior petals, protruding at the tip. The leaves are large, light green, and much divided.

The plant has reddish buds in early spring, coming into flower a little later and fading after about a month. It then turns yellow and shrivels up, and all the top growth completely disappears in the summer.

*Dicentra* prospers in a nourishing, light soil with plenty of moisture in spring. It grows best in mild half-shade, but it can also stand sunshine.

It is not used in mixed borders, where its special beauty would be lost. It stands out well as a solitary plant, especially against a darker background of conifers. They also give it some protection from cold winds for, although the plant is hardy, the foliage is liable to damage. Creeping or dwarf perennials can be used as a setting. They are particularly suitable as not only do they blend well with Bleeding Heart, but they also camouflage the empty space which appears after it has died down.

It is propagated by division of root segments or by cuttings.

*Dicentra spectabilis*

## Ajuga
BUGLE
10—20 cms (4—8 ins); V—VI

Labiatae
The Mint Family

Bugle is a small perennial, which is especially cultivated for its attractive leaves. It forms thick, weed-suppressing growths, which can be well used in ornamental gardens. It forms straight stalks, up to 30 cms (12 ins) high, in the flowering season from May to July, which carry a dense spike of gentian-blue, tubular, lipped flowers. After flowering it is useful to cut away the dying stalks. The pleasant foliage of Bugle, which lasts throughout the winter is a feature in the garden all year round.

The most important Bugles planted in gardens are the following: *Ajuga reptans* which has oval variegated leaves of reddish-bronze and gay yellow. *A. r.* var. *multicoloris* 'Rainbow' has brown, green, red and yellow-flecked leaves. Another Bugle *A. r. fol. argenteis* has gay, white leaves. *A. r. atropurpurea* has bronze-red leaves; blue-flowering plants show up particularly well when combined with this form.

Bugle thrives best in a reasonably damp, sandy soil. The most suitable situation is in mild, semi-shade.

It is as suitable for rockeries as for borders and as a carpeting plant in informal groups. It has occasionally been used as a lawn substitute, where there are suitable soil conditions with the right amount of moisture. It adapts well and can be very invasive. It is easily propagated by division. It throws off leafy runners from the main stems which root easily and can be planted at intervals of 30 cms (12 ins).

*Ajuga reptans*

# *Brunnera myosotidiflora*　　Boraginaceae
The Borage Family

20—30 cms (8—12 ins); V—VI

*Brunnera* forms bushy plants which grow up to 30 cms (12 ins) high and are thickly covered with heart-shaped, hairy leaves. Its sprays of fine blue flowers reminiscent of Forget-me-nots, rise up above the leaves during the main flowering season from late April to June, but individual flowers develop throughout the summer although not in such profusion. Even after the flowers fade away, the plant is a decorative feature for it holds its leaves almost until winter. It buds in spring at the end of April, and because its roots are not too thick and strong-growing, it can be used with success as an in-between-plant among various spring bulbs, which flower in March and at the beginning of April. They do not obstruct one another and when the bulbs die off, *Brunnera* covers up the seemingly empty space.

It grows best in partial shade, but it also grows in full sun and in complete shade. The soil should be humous and reasonably moist. Dry conditions are not favourable.

It is a very valuable and rewarding perennial. It can be used in larger rockeries, in borders, in informal groups especially of spring flowers, such as Leopard's Bane, Globe Flower, Hellebore, etc.

It is propagated from seed or cuttings about 10—12 cms (4—5 ins) long, which should be taken in late autumn. They should then be put in boxes so that they can pass the winter without fear of being killed off by frost, and can later be planted out at intervals of 40 cms (16 ins).

The plant lives for many years and does not require any special care.

*Brunnera myosotidiflora*

## *Dianthus*

Caryophyllaceae

PINK, CARNATION

The Pink Family

20—30 cms (8—12 ins); V—VI

Pinks are plants of an old culture, cultivated in gardens for many centuries and popular for their beautiful blossoms and fragrance. The genus *Dianthus* is very rich in annuals, biennials and perennials. The most valuable perennial species for use in the garden are those which in addition to providing attractive flowers over a long period, form very decorative clumps of permanent silvery-blue or green foliage.

*Dianthus plumarius*, the Cottage Pink, is one of the most well-known garden Pinks and forms large, thick cushions of narrow blue-green leaves. It has a profusion of quite large flowers, either single or double, in various colours, from white and pink through to red. By far the most popular 'Pinks' in British gardens are *D. caryophyllus*, the Border Carnations, tough hardy perennials of great beauty which have been much hybridized and are available in many named cultivars.

Pinks are very resistant perennials, quite modest in their requirements. They love warmth, sun and rather dry conditions, with a well-drained and calcareous soil. In winter they can be harmed by damp.

The beautiful grey-blue cushions of their needle leaves are suitable for borders, rockeries, dry walls, and are as welcome as an evergreen of creeping growth in informally planted groups. Varieties with large double flowers are suitable for cutting.

It is usually propagated by 'slips' (cuttings) between July and August. Single varieties are easily propagated from seed in spring. It should be planted at intervals of 30 cms (12 ins).

*Dianthus plumarius*

# *Digitalis*

FOXGLOVE

80—150 cms (2½—5 ft); V—VI

Scrophulariaceae

The Foxglove Family

This is a well-known plant with bell-shaped flowers decoratively arranged in a long spike on an upright stalk. The leaves are deep green and lance-shaped and form quite a large basal rosette, but smaller leaves also grow directly from the flower stems. The whole Foxglove plant contains poisonous alkaloids — digitoxin and digitalin — which are an important constituent of heart medicines. Foxglove was originally, therefore, cultivated as a medicinal herb.

The best-known is *Digitalis purpurea* with light purple-red flowers. This fundamental type, which also grows wild, is grown particularly for pharmaceutical purposes, but *D. purpurea* 'Gloxiniaeflora' has some standing as a decorative plant. It has larger flowering and denser spikes with the flowers arranged right round the stem. The range of colours is also richer including pure white, cream, light pink, carmine and deep purple. Foxgloves have no special requirements as to soil, provided it is not too heavy and wet.

Foxglove is used in mixed formal flower-beds with perennials and annuals, and also in wild gardens and as contrast among cushions of low grasses and trailing plants. In effect it is a biennial plant, which means that it forms a large leaf rosette in the first year after sowing, from which the flowering stalks grow only in the second year.

It is propagated exclusively from seed which should be sown at the end of May or at the beginning of June, transplanted and moved to permanent positions in September at intervals of 50 cms (20 ins).

*Digitalis purpurea* 'Gloxiniaeflora'

84

# *Euphorbia*

SPURGE, MILKWORT

40—50 cms (16—20 ins); V—VI

Euphorbiaceae

The Spurge Family

Typically characteristic of Spurges are the milk-like sap, which drips from half-broken stalks, and the inconspicuous flowers, which are overshadowed by striking yellow leaves. Some Spurges are planted in gardens as ornamental plants; *Euphorbia polychroma (E. epithymoides)* is one of the most valuable of these. It forms thick clumps with elongated leaves covered with fine hairs. Rosettes of deep yellow leaves, which look like flowers, develop at the end of the purplish-green shoots in the flowering season in April. The plant is attractive throughout the year; its leaves turn orange-red in autumn.

It grows well in full sunshine and even half-shade. It grows in any calcareous soil, but best of all in a dry and warm situation. If the soil is too rich and wet the plants grow leggy and flop about after the flowers fade; they lose their compact shape and their decorative value is diminished.

This is a very hardy plant, which will remain in one place for many years and still produce a beautiful display. It is an ideal subject for rockeries, and can also be used as a solitary, or near the foreground in herbaceous borders, on the top of garden walls and as an edging plant. But it is most useful in naturally planted groups of low-growing or creeping perennials thriving in dry conditions.

Spurge is propagated by division, or by pieces torn away in early spring and in summer, or by summer cuttings. It is propagated equally well from seed sown in spring. The plants should be placed 40—50 cms (16—20 ins) apart.

*Euphorbia polychroma*

# *Lupinus*

LUPIN

70—100 cms (2¼—3 ft); V—VI

Leguminosae

The Pea Family

The Lupin is a popular plant with handsome foliage. The leaves are palmate and form a thick bush, from which several strong, hollow stalks grow in the flowering season, terminating in a dense spike of blossom. It flowers at the end of May and in June. If the dead flowerheads are cut off immediately after fading, the plant usually flowers again at the end of the summer.

*Lupinus polyphyllus*, the common blue wild species, originally came from North America. George Russell, the English grower, developed beautifully coloured hybrids by crossbreeding which today constitute an important group of varieties called Russell Lupins.

*L. polyphyllus* is very undemanding and will grow in practically any soil in either sunshine or half-shade. It is propagated easily from seed, and also seeds itself very readily.

Russell Lupins, however, are far more demanding. They require good deep soil, which is neither too dry nor too wet, and with a neutral or slightly acid reaction. They also require a sunny position.

Individual groups of one or more colours are especially beautiful when planted in large quantities or, for example, yellow Lupins could be combined with Oriental Poppies, Irises and Paeonies. They are also a beautiful plant for cutting.

The varieties can be propagated vegetatively by cuttings, but the procedure is quite difficult. Propagation from seed is far easier. Lupins should be planted at intervals of 50—60 cms (1½—2 ft).

Russell Lupin

## *Papaver*

POPPY

40—80 cms (1¼—2¼ ft); V—VI

Papaveraceae

The Poppy Family

Poppies are flowers which excel in the brilliance of their colouring, but usually they do not last long.

*Papaver orientale* is one of the most long-lived. It comes from the Caucasus and northern Iran. It is a handsome plant with long, straight, fleshy roots. It forms big rosettes of large, dark green, elongated, deeply toothed leaves and the whole plant is covered with rough hairs. The large, single or semi-double flowers are usually a flashing red, with a large black fleck at the base of each petal and prominent black stamens. The seed is contained in the large and decorative poppy-head. The plant flowers from the end of May, but its main season is in June. When the flowers fade away, it shrivels up, so that by the end of June and in July all its top growth has disappeared. It buds again in autumn and forms low rosettes of leaves during winter.

Many beautiful varieties have been developed, especially in England and Germany, with flowers ranging from red, orange and pink to white.

The Oriental Poppy needs sunshine and a nourishing, well-drained soil. It is very durable and contrasts well with other plants. It lasts a long time in one spot almost without attention.

It is a beautiful solitary plant for the lawn and can also be used in mixed groups.

It is propagated principally by root cuttings from December until February. It can also be sown, but seed-grown plants do not have the characteristics of the parent: they are noticeably taller and leggier. The planting distance is 60 cms (2 ft).

*Papaver orientale*

## *Saponaria*

SOAPWORT

10—30 cms (4—12 ins); V—VI

Caryophyllaceae

The Pink Family

There are several species of Soapwort; those which are low-growing and form thick cushion-like growths covered with flowers, are of most use in the garden. *Saponaria ocymoides* is the species most often seen. It is a rock plant which grows freely on the southern slopes of the Alps, up to a height of 2,000 metres (6,000 ft). It develops large, overhanging cushions 10—30 cms (4—12 ins) high and up to 1 metre (3 ft) wide. Its many-branched stems with small, oval leaves terminate in a number of small pinky-carmine flowers from the second half of May until June. It often flowers again from August to September.

Apart from the species, some other varieties are also cultivated. *S. ocymoides* var. *splendens* is a variety with larger, vibrant pinky-red flowers. *S. o.* var. *alba* has white flowers, but it is not so striking as the former.

Soapwort grows well in any dry, calcareous, sandy soil in a sunny place. It cannot stand damp conditions.

It thrives best of all on top of dry walls, where it spreads profusely, cascading over the stonework. It also provides beautiful patches of colour in the rockery, especially when grown with Sun Roses, Speedwells, etc. It forms attractive cushions in freely planted groups in dry sunny places.

It is propagated easily from seed; in suitable places it even seeds spontaneously. Plants can also be divided. It should be planted at intervals of 30—40 cms (12—16 ins).

*Saponaria ocymoides*

## *Trollius*                                    Ranunculaceae
GLOBE FLOWER                           The Buttercup Family
40—80 cms (1¼—2½ ft); V—VI

Globe Flowers grow wild in damp meadows. The yellow globular
flowers are borne singly on tall branching stems above the deeply
divided palmate foliage. The bushy plants are 40—60 cms
(16—24 ins) high. European Globe Flowers have been crossbred
with Chinese and Asiatic Globe Flowers, and thus hybrid varieties
have been developed, which are now cultivated in our gardens as
attractive and satisfying spring perennials. *Trollius* × *cultorum*
'Aetna' is dark orange, 70 cms (2¼ ft) high; *T.* × *c.* 'Alabaster' is
cream-white, 20 cms (8 ins) shorter. *T.* × *c.* 'Golden Queen' has
large yellow-orange flowers on stems 60—70 cms (2—2¼ ft) high.
*T.* × *c.* 'Prichard's Giant' is golden-orange and robust, an early
Globe Flower which reaches a height of 80—90 cms (2½—3 ft).

Globe Flowers are spring perennials noted for their versatility.
Garden varieties do not need a damp, acid soil like their parents.
Average garden conditions satisfy them quite well, but they will
not tolerate wet conditions and, moreover, need a sunny position.
If all the dead heads are cut away immediately after flowering, the
plants will often flower again.

Globe Flowers can be used either in formal flower-beds among
medium-sized groups of spring perennials, or in wild gardens.
They adapt very well to growing beside water, either planted in
firm banks or in the mud at the edge of ponds and small lakes.
The plants are very hardy and disease-resistant.

They are easily propagated by division, which is best carried out
in early autumn. They should be planted at intervals of 30—40 cms
(12—16 ins).

*Trollius* × *cultorum*

94

# *Viscaria vulgaris*

CAMPION

30—40 cms (12—16 ins); V—VI

Caryophyllaceae

The Pink Family

Some nurseries grow this beautiful plant under the name of *Lychnis viscaria*. *Viscaria vulgaris* 'Splendens Plena', a double form of Campion, is the variety mainly found in gardens.

The plant forms tufts of long, narrow lanceolate leaves, reminiscent of Carnations in the flowering season. It has large, double, glossy carmine-pink flowers arranged in a spike at the end of the stalks. *V. vulgaris* 'Fontane' is a variety with a more vigorous growth and large flowers, a little lighter in colour. A white form also exists, but it is not as attractive as the pink. The Campion loves a sunny position and a good humous soil, which should not be too dry; it cannot stand wet conditions. It is not a long-lasting perennial. It is necessary to pull up the plants, divide and transplant them in fresh soil in their fourth or fifth year, if not sooner. After the flowers have faded, it is a good idea to feed the plants with a balanced fertilizer.

Campions are suitable for formal flower-beds, where their shiny colour is very effective, particularly next to blue-coloured perennials. Clumps of Campions also look well growing with grey narrow-leaved grasses like *Festuca glauca* and in association with dwarf creeping plants in informal groups. It is also suitable for cutting, though the flowers do not last particularly long.

It is propagated by division. The most suitable time for doing this is after the flowers have died. The new plants should be set out at intervals of 35 cms (14 ins).

*Viscaria vulgaris*

# *Iris*

IRIS

60—100 cms (2—3 ft); V—VII

Iridaceae

The Iris Family

Irises are a very extensive family, found nearly all the world over. Most varieties cultivated in gardens are hybrids of various types; the pure species are not so commonly grown.

One of the most important groups of Irises is known today under the name of *Iris germanica*, the Tall Bearded or Flag Iris. Plants of this group are 50—100 cms (1½—3 ft) high. They flower from the end of May until July and the flowers cover a wide range of colours. It is a pity that their flowering period does not last longer. There is an inexhaustible number of varieties and new ones are added every year. Some of the more important are listed below: *I. germanica* 'Blue Valley' is light blue with an orange fall, while *I. g.* 'White City' has large white flowers with wavy edges and yellow falls. *I. g.* 'Ola Kala' is a deep, golden-yellow. *I. g.* 'Prairie Sunset' has large blossoms of blended red, pink, apricot and peach shades. *I. g.* 'Sable' is one of the darkest varieties with deep. purple-black flowers.

The new varieties are more particular than the old ones as to their requirements. They need a deep, nourishing, well-drained soil, a sunny position or light, half-shade. They suffer from damp rot in heavy soil or in excessively rainy years.

Irises can be used in mixed formal flower-beds, but best of all, planted in groups of varieties with complementary colours in association with smaller perennials having a different flowering season.

They are easily propagated by division of the rhizomes; only the youngest segments should be used. The best time for division is after the flowers fade away, or in early autumn, so that they can root before winter. They should be planted at intervals of 40 cms (16 ins).

*Iris germanica*

## *Polygonatum*
SOLOMON'S SEAL
50—150 cms (1½—5 ft); V—VII

Liliaceae
The Lily Family

This is a plant coming from light forest regions. It has strong, white creeping rhizomes and, above ground, long arching stems bearing oval leaves, set either in pairs or alternately, and pendent white and green bell-shaped flowers. The roots were used for medicinal purposes in the past.

The two garden species mainly cultivated are: *Polygonatum commutatum* and *P. multiflorum*. *P. commutatum (P. giganteum)* is a strong-growing plant, up to 150 cms (5 ft) high, which originated in North America. The leaves on the stalk are up to 20 cms (8 ins) long and the flowers are grouped in tens. They are about 2 cms (¾ in.) long, white, with green flecks at the edges, and are in bloom from May until July. *P. commutatum* grows profusely in suitable conditions and needs quite a lot of space. It is seen to best advantage planted in groups with a carpet of shade-loving perennials of cushiony growth. *P. multiflorum* is a smaller plant, only about 50—90 cms (1½—3 ft) high. The stalks, leafless at the base, have alternate, lance-shaped leaves, up to 15 cms (6 ins) long, grey-green on the underside. The flowers are arranged in ones to sixes and are greenish-white. It flowers from May to June.

It thrives best in a deep, humous soil which is not too dry, but it can be adversely affected by wet conditions. A half-shaded to shady position should be selected for it.

Solomon's Seal can easily be propagated in spring or in autumn by division. The divisions of the rhizomes should be at least 10 cms (4 ins) long. It is also possible to grow it from seed, but it takes a long time for the plants to reach maturity. They should be planted at intervals of 60—80 cms (2—2½ ft).

*Polygonatum multiflorum*

## *Veronica*

Scrophulariaceae

The Foxglove Family

The genus *Veronica* is a very rich one; most species have blue flowers and they have a very wide use in the garden. But individual species differ from each other in height and colour. Low-growing types are most valuable. *Veronica incana* is very attractive with silvery-grey foliage arranged in large rosettes, which merge together to form widespread carpets. It bears fine dark blue spikes of flowers about 20—30 cms (8—12 ins) high from mid-June to July. It is suitable for rockeries and borders and as a carpeter in informal groups. Another species, *V. teucrium*, forms thick bushes, 20—30 cms (8—12 ins) high, covered with a profusion of blue flowers from May until July. Several excellent varieties have been cultivated. *V. teucrium* 'Royal Blue' is 25—30 cms (10—12 ins) high, gentian-blue and very vigorous. Another variety *V. t.* 'Shirley Blue' has abundant flowers of a shimmering blue and is 25 cms (10 ins) high.

Another rather tall species of Speedwell is *V. spicata*. The flowering plant is 30—40 cms (12—16 ins) high, with elongated leaves covered with fine greyish hair. It produces handsome, up-right, spiky flowerheads in July. Particularly popular varieties are: *V. spicata* 'Rosea Erika' which is a dark pink variety, about 30 cms (12 ins) high, and *V. s.* 'Romiley Purple' which is a shiny purple-blue and about 40 cms (16 ins) high.

Speedwells do not have any particular requirements; they are content in any garden soil, and love sunshine. They are used in rockeries, for borders and in general perennial groups. Bushy species can also be used in mixed formal flower-beds.

It is easily propagated by division and also by cuttings. It should be planted at intervals of 25—35 cms (10—14 ins).

*Veronica incana*

## *Achillea*

### MILFOIL, YARROW

Various heights and flowering seasons

Compositae

The Daisy Family

The genus *Achillea* in the wild is widespread and includes a great number of species. Many Milfoils are planted in gardens for their decorative value and wide range of uses. Among them, there are low-growing prostrate forms, which are invaluable in rockeries and as carpeting plants in informal groups; others of medium height are suitable for herbaceous borders, for cutting, etc., and tall varieties can be similarly used.

*Achillea serbica* and *A. tomentosa* are the best prostrate Milfoils. *A. serbica*, 15—20 cms (6—8 ins) tall [V—VI], has narrow, silvery, felt-like leaves which last through winter. The flowers are white and relatively large. It is one of the most beautiful and satisfying Milfoils. *A. tomentosa*, 10—15 cms (4—6 ins) tall [VI—VII], is a carpeting plant with silvery, hairy leaves, markedly subdivided. The flowers are golden-yellow in crested racemes.

Both Milfoils require a sunny position and thrive best in a light, dry soil. They are easily propagated by division or by cuttings. They are suitable for rockeries and garden walls and should be planted at intervals of 25 cms (10 ins).

*A. filipendulina*, 100—150 cms (3—5 ft) tall [VII—VIII], belongs to the tallest group of Milfoils. It forms large clumps of ferny foliage from which rise tall, stiff stems bearing at their tips large, thick clusters of small, closely-packed golden-yellow flowers. *A. f.* 'Parker's Variety' is the tallest; it measures 120—150 cms (4—5 ft). *A. f.* 'Gold Plate' is the most popular.

The requirements as to soil, position and propagation are the same as for the small Milfoils, but they should be planted at intervals of 50 cms (20 ins).

*Achillea filipendulina* 'Parker's Variety'

104

# *Geum*

AVENS

30—60 cms (1—2 ft); V—VIII

Rosaceae

The Rose Family

Avens are small to medium tall perennials with striking, vibrantly coloured flowers. The leaves are dark green, lobed and form thick clumps. The saucer-shaped blossoms are single or semi-double, set singly on branching stalks. Many varieties are often very similar to each other, but the following are among the most beautiful: *Geum chiloense* has a bushy habit, with branching stems about 60 cm (2 ft) high. The leaves are much divided into ten or twelve sections. The blossoms, about 3 cms (1 in.) across, are scarlet-red. I gradually comes into flower in May and then often continues right up until the end of August. *G. ch.* 'Mrs. Bradshaw', a variety of this sub-group, has intense scarlet, semi-double blossoms. *G. ch.* 'Goldball' is a variety similar to the latter, but with yellow flowers.

*Geum* has been much hybridized and is cultivated under the type name. *G.* 'Fire Opal' is a variety with orange-scarlet semi-double flowers, 50 cms (20 ins) high; *G.* 'Princess Juliana' has semi-double blossoms which are a shining orange-yellow and reach a height of 50 cms (20 ins). *G.* 'Red Wings' is a luminous, translucent red semi-double variety, about 30—40 cms (12—16 ins) high.

Avens like sunny positions and a permeable humous soil. Because of their lively colours they are suitable for multi-coloured formal beds, for borders and for natural groups. The blossoms soon fall, but new ones continually replace them.

They are propagated by division in early spring. Plants at least two years old are most suitable for division. Some varieties can also be propagated from seed. They should be planted at intervals of 30—40 cms (12—16 ins).

*Geum chiloense* 'Mrs. Bradshaw'

# *Hemerocallis*
DAY LILY
40—100 cms (1¼—3 ft); V—VIII

Liliaceae

The Lily Family

The Day Lily, an attractive perennial with long, narrow, grace-fully arching foliage, has lily-like flowers arranged in branched flowerheads at the top of long leafless stalks. Although the flowers only last a day, they appear in unfailing succession so that the plant is in flower for at least a month. They are yellow, orange and apricot, and new varieties are even red and pink in colour.

*Hemerocallis fulva* is a species which grows profusely. It is 80—100 cms (2½—3 ft) high, with brownish-orange flowers from June to August. *H. citrina* is also later. Its clear yellow flowers are on long stalks 120 cms (4 ft) tall. The deep yellow Day Lily, *H. middendorfii*, is the smallest, only 40—50 cms (16—20 ins) tall, and it is also the earliest.

Under the name of *H. hybrida*, varieties are introduced which have been developed by crossbreeding. They contain many clear colours, especially shades of red and pink.

Day Lilies are beautiful and undemanding perennials which give a great deal of pleasure. They grow well in full sunshine and in dry conditions. They prefer a deep, nourishing soil and grow less satisfactorily only where the soil is poor and sandy.

They stand out well in mixed borders and they are perhaps best used as solitaries and in natural groups with small perennials.

Day Lilies are easily propagated by division in spring. They can be left without lifting for a long time in one place and will still flower profusely. They should be planted at intervals of 50 cms (20 ins).

*Hemerocallis citrina*

## *Nepeta*

CATMINT

30 cms (1 ft); V—IX

Labiatae

The Mint Family

Catmint with its thick bushes of grey-green aromatic foliage comes from the dry mountain pastures of the Caucasus and Asia Minor. It has small heart-shaped leaves with serrated edges. Tiny, lavender-blue tubular flowers cluster in bunches at the axil point of the leaves right up the stem.

*Nepeta mussini* is most often cultivated. It is about 30 cms (12 ins) high and has light purple flowers from June to August. *N. faassenii* forms upright bushes and is also taller, about 40—50 cms (16—20 ins), with blue-purple flowers from May until September. *N. f.* 'Six Hills Giant' is a variety up to 60 cms (2 ft) high with larger lilac blossoms. It also flowers over a long period and has a wild form.

Catmints are perennials designed for dry conditions and sunny places. They do not have any special requirements as to soil except that it should be well drained. They are very valuable perennials for dry places, larger rockeries, borders, dry walls and naturally planted groups. Their lengthy flowering season is very valuable, and with *N. mussini* it can be prolonged if the plants are trimmed near the end of the first flowering. They then bud again and are in flower almost until winter.

Catmint is an important plant for bee-keepers. It is propagated by division early in spring and should be planted at intervals of 30 cms (12 ins).

*Nepeta mussini*

110

# *Viola cornuta*

HORNED PANSY, VIOLA

15—20 cms (6—8 ins); V—X

Violaceae

The Violet Family

*Viola cornuta* is a relative of our well-known biennial, the Pansy. It differs in that it has a smaller flower and that it is a perennial. In suitable conditions it flowers profusely from spring almost until the first frost in a kaleidoscopic range of colours from white to purple-black.

*Viola cornuta* is the most important of perennial Pansies. It comes from the Pyrenees; it is about 15—20 cms (6—8 ins) high and in time forms wide-spreading growths. The blossoms are 3—5 cms (1—2 ins) across, ranging in colour from white, cream-yellow and pale lilac to blue and dark purple. It has a number of varieties. *V. cornuta* 'Amethyst' is a deep purple with large flowers; *V. c.* 'Altona' is cream-yellow. The blue flowers of *V. c.* 'Blauwunder' with their purple sheen really glisten and flower for a long time. *V. c.* 'White Superior' is white with large flowers and *V. c.* 'Velvet Beauty' is of a velvet, purple-black colour.

The majority of varieties have their main flowering season from May to June, followed by a short resting period, and start flowering again from mid-summer until autumn. It is one of the longest flowering perennials and therefore particularly appreciated.

It needs the right conditions to reveal itself in its full beauty: a permeable, humous soil which is not too rich. It cannot stand scorching heat and dryness or a damp, heavy shade.

It is widely used in rockeries, on flower walls, and for hanging baskets and pots.

It is propagated by division or cuttings. Some varieties kept by growers can even be seeded. It should be planted at intervals of 30 cms (12 ins).

*Viola cornuta* 'Amethyst'

## *Aruncus*

GOAT'S BEARD

120—150 cms (4—5 ft); VI

Rosaceae

The Rose Family

This beautiful plant originally came from shady clearings in damp mountain forests; because of its beauty it has been cultivated as a garden species. It grows well in cultivation and if suitably used can become a decorative feature of every garden.

In fact only *Aruncus silvester* is of any use for cultivation in gardens. It is a large plant, which will only attain its full height if left for several years without being disturbed. It grows up to 150 cms (5 ft) high. Its pinnate leaves are up to 50 cms (20 ins) long. The plant forms a clump, which in the flowering season has a number of stalks terminating in branched racemes of fine, cream-white flowers, a little reminiscent of *Astilbe* in shape. These flowering racemes are held well above the leaves, so that the whole flowering plant, especially when older, is very ornamental.

Goat's Beard is not very demanding as to soil, although it thrives best in a slightly humous soil with a fair amount of moisture. It grows well in half-shade, and even in sun if the soil is sufficiently damp. It cannot, however, stand persistent dampness. It lives for many years in an appropriate situation and needs scarcely any attention.

Its principal use is in wild gardens and parks in solitary groups. It looks marvellous in combination with Delphiniums. It is also very well adapted for cutting and for adding lightness to bouquets.

It is propagated either from seed or by division; the best time for this is at the end of summer and beginning of autumn. It should be planted at intervals of 80—100 cms (2½—3 ft).

*Aruncus silvester*

# *Paeonia*

PAEONY

60—100 cms (2—3 ft); VI

Ranunculaceae
The Buttercup Family

This is a plant with an ancient lineage which originated in China and Japan, where many varieties were cultivated. It was introduced into Europe in the 18th century and the number of its varieties is today counted in thousands.

*Paeonia lactiflora* is the most cultivated and one of the most important species for gardens. Some of the more valuable varieties from the inexhaustible list follow: *P. lactiflora* 'Adolphe Rousseau' is dark red and early; *P. l.* 'Bunker Hill' is light red and early; *P. l.* 'Lord Kitchener' is salmon-pink and flowers in mid-June; *P. l.* 'Avalanche' is ivory-white and late.

The main flowering season is June; the early varieties start flowering as early as the end of May, the late ones flower until July. In addition to their spectacular beauty, Paeonies are very undemanding. They thrive best in sunshine in a nourishing, deep garden soil. They can be left in one place for many years almost without attention and in fact resent disturbance. They respond very well to an occasional mulch with manure or compost.

They are most suited to being planted in solitary groups among trees and shrubs. The Paeony is also an important flower for cutting purposes. They can be cut while in bud and will open up in the vase and last quite a long time.

They are propagated by division of the tuberous roots, but the gardener must make sure that each divided tuber has an 'eye' or bud, similar to that on a Dahlia. Paeonies should be transplanted and divided in the autumn, when the plant is dormant. Seedlings do not flower when planted deep. The buds on the tuber should not be deeper in the ground than 3 cms (1¼ ins). They should be planted at intervals of 50 cms (20 ins).

*Paeonia lactiflora*

# *Aquilegia*

COLUMBINE

50—70 cms (1¾—2½ ft); VI—VII

Ranunculaceae

The Buttercup Family

The Columbine was cultivated in gardens many years ago as a rewarding, undemanding perennial with flowers in pink, purple and white shades. Thanks especially to American cultivators, unprecedented colours have recently appeared in Columbines. Their blossoms are larger, with longer and slimmer spurs and even two-toned. They are hybrids, developed by crossbreeding, and are called *Aquilegia hybrida*. They are about 50—70 cms (1½—2¼ ft) high with blue-green subdivided leaves from which branched stalks spring up at the end of May and mainly in June, carrying individual flowers. At least four of these jewel-like newer varieties must be mentioned: *A. hybrida* 'Crimson Star' has petals with vibrant red spurs, its sepals are white to cream; *A. h.* 'Edelweiss' is pure white, with large flowers; *A. h.* 'Star of India' has orange-red petals and deep yellow sepals; *A. h.* 'Rose Queen' is pure pink.

The soil for Columbines should be a reasonably moist humus. They prefer a light half-shade and will not do so well if they are exposed to the scorching heat of the sun and placed in a dry location.

Columbines are delicate flowers, whose beauty is lost at a distance. They are not used, therefore, for great massive effects, but rather in groups near paths where they can be observed closely. They are best employed in informal groups, especially with a background of darker conifers.

Columbines are propagated mainly from seed, but named varieties are propagated by division in autumn. They are planted at intervals of 40 cms (16 ins).

*Aquilegia hybrida*

# *Campanula persicifolia*

BELLFLOWER

50—80 cms (1½—2½ ft); VI—VII

Campanulaceae

The Bellflower Family

Bellflowers are an extensive group of flowers and can be seen in gardens in numerous different species and varieties, but particularly as low-growing rockery plants; they are indispensable in all rockeries. There are also beautiful taller Bellflowers, which are useful in perennial groups and for cutting. *Campanula persicifolia* is without question one of the most beautiful of these. It forms a ground rosette of narrow leaves, from which a cluster of slender stems grows in the flowering season, each bearing three to five large, shallow chalice-like blossoms. They are lavender-blue in colour, and when wide open about 4 cms (1½ ins) in diameter. *C. persicifolia* has several varieties: *C. persicifolia* 'Alba' has white single blossoms and is 70 cms (2¼ ft) high; *C. p.* 'Misty Morn' has semi-double, light blue bells and a height of 50—60 cms (1½—2 ft); *C. p.* 'Moerheimii' is a variety with semi-double white flowers 50—70 cms (1½—2¼ ft); *C. p.* 'Telham Beauty' has large, dark blue blossoms. The height is 60—80 cms (2—2½ ft).

Warm, nourishing, well-drained soil is the most suitable for these Bellflowers. Even if they can stand sunshine, they thrive best in half-shade.

It is a valuable perennial for mixed groups and borders, and is also suitable for cutting and the wild garden. It combines well, for instance, with Columbines.

The original species can be propagated from seed, otherwise all can be propagated easily by division of their clumps. They should be planted at intervals of 40 cms (16 ins).

*Campanula persicifolia*

# *Delphinium*

DELPHINIUM

120—180 cms (4—6 ft); VI—VII

Ranunculaceae

The Buttercup Family

Delphinium is a very attractive perennial, forming large, bushy plants with dense flower spikes up to 180 cms (6 ft) in height, usually of blue florets with 'eyes', but their colour range includes all shades of blue and purple to pink and white. The main flowering season is June until mid-July. If the faded flowerheads are cut off in time, Delphiniums flower again in autumn.

Hybrids, which have been cultivated in great numbers, are of uncertain lineage but probably they are derived from *Delphinium elatum*. Of the varieties, mention must be made of: *D.* 'Blue Beauty' which is gentian-blue with a black eye, 150 cms (5 ft) high; another is *D.* 'Gute Nacht', which is semi-double, dark blue and purple with a white eye, 130—150 cms (4½—5 ft) high; *D.* 'Moerheimii' is pure white, semi-double, 120 cms (4 ft) high and *D.* 'Wild Wales' which is gentian-blue and pink with a black eye and is 180 cms (6 ft) high.

Delphiniums are fastidious perennials. The soil should be a deep, loose, well-fertilized humus adequately moistened. The position should be sunny and sheltered from the wind, which can easily break and uproot flowering plants. Occasional feeding with liquid manure is very beneficial. The plants will live for as long as ten years in one position, but it is better to divide and transplant the clumps after five or six years. They can be planted as solitaries or in informal groups with smaller perennials or to the rear of mixed borders.

Propagation by division in spring is very easy. Propagation from seed is also easy, but does not maintain the characteristics of the parent. If sown in spring, the young plants flower in the same year. Delphiniums should be planted at intervals of 70—80 cms (2¼—2½ ft).

*Delphinium elatum*

# *Dictamnus*

BURNING BUSH

70—100 cms (2¼—3 ft); VI—VII

Rutaceae

The Rue Family

This is an interesting and decorative plant native to the temperate zones of Europe and Asia. It forms tufts of tough stalks with large feathery leaves. The flowers are arranged in thin clusters above the leaves. They are pink or white, with distinctive venation. The whole plant smells strongly of lemon and formerly the oils which produce this smell were used medicinally.

*Dictamnus albus* is a species with bushes about 1 metre (3 ft) high and pink-veined flowers. There are several varieties; for instance *D. a.* var. *albiflorus*, with pure white blossoms, or *D. a.* var. *ruber*, with carmine-pink flowers.

The plant flowers from June to July. It thrives best in a warm, sunny place with a nourishing, calcareous soil, and can withstand dry conditions very well. Burning Bush is a very durable and long-lived plant and it seeds itself.

It is attractive not only for its flowers but also for its foliage and its entire manner of growth. It is at its best growing in groups among low clumps of *Festuca*, Thyme, yellow Flax, Stonecrop, *Antennaria dioica*, etc. It also looks well growing in isolated clumps round the lawn.

It is propagated from seed, which should be sown immediately after ripening. Plants should be moved while still small as older ones do not stand up to transplanting very well. Burning Bush grows quite slowly, and when seed-grown it takes three or four years before it starts flowering. It should be planted at intervals of 80—100 cms (2½—3 ft).

*Dictamnus albus*

# *Eremurus*

FOXTAIL LILY

80—250 cms (2½—8 ft); VI—VII

Liliaceae

The Lily Family

In spring the Foxtail Lily throws out ground rosettes of narrow leaves, from which in June and July a tall stalk grows bearing at its tip a long, thick cluster of pink, white, yellow or orange star-like blossoms with remarkable stamens. The plant originally came from the Asiatic steppes, and its main vegetation period is spring. After the flowers fade away, it quickly shrivels up so that by the beginning of summer all its leaves have completely disappeared. Three species are most commonly cultivated. *Eremurus robustus*, in which the flowerhead reaches a height of 180—250 cms (6—8 ft), is the largest; the blossoms are light pink. *E. himalaicus* is smaller, 100—150 cms (3—5 ft), and its white blossoms are arranged in a spike up to 80 cms (2½ ft) long. *E. stenophyllus* 'Bungei' is 80—120 cms (2½—4 ft) high, with deep yellow flowers of which the stamens have reddish anthers.

Hybrids of these species appear in the shops under the description Shelford Hybrids with such variety names as: 'Citronelle', which is sulphur-yellow; 'Flair', golden-yellow with a particularly long flower spike; 'Lady Felmontz', brownish-orange; 'Rosalind', a warm lilac-pink; and 'White Beauty', an early, pure white variety.

Foxtail Lilies should be planted in a sunny, warm, protected location, in deep, nourishing, well-drained soil. They can stand up to dryness very well, but must have moisture in spring; otherwise damp conditions are harmful, particularly after the flowers fade away and during winter.

The plant is very attractive and especially suitable for isolated use in groups of five to seven plants. It is propagated primarily by seed; vegetative propagation of the varieties must be by careful division of the roots. It should be planted at intervals of 50—60 cms (20—24 ins).

*Eremurus stenophyllus* 'Bungei'

126

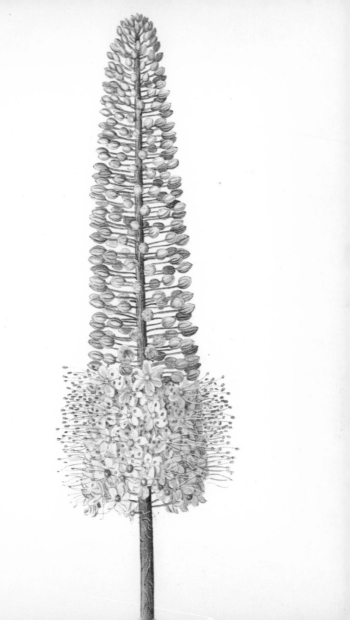

# *Eryngium*

SEA HOLLY

30—100 cms (1—3 ft); VI—VII

Umbelliferae

The Hemlock Family

In appearance these plants are reminiscent of the thistle, though they are not related to it at all. The tough leaves are prickly yet decorative, subdivided, and have various types of venation. The tiny florets are arranged in cones, which are surrounded by a rosette of prickly leaves. Some of the Sea Hollies have these flower cones in blue, others in silvery-green. Many species are widespread in very dry, sandy, barren places. Some of them are cultivated as decorative perennials for a specific purpose.

*Eryngium alpinum* is a plant 50—60 cms (20--24 ins) high with blue flowers and spiky, bluish leaves. It blooms from June to July and has several forms which differ in the height and colour of the flowerheads. *E. bourgatii* is 40—50 cms (16—20 ins) tall. Its leaves are very delicately subdivided, with prominent white venation. The flower cone is bluish with a collar of finely divided, long, narrow leaves. *E. oliveranum* is 70—80 cms (2¼—2½ ft) tall with a number of small cones. The whole plant is steel blue.

All Sea Hollies are very undemanding; they will thrive in a poor, sandy soil provided it has sufficient lime and is in full sun. It is suitable for growing against a darker background among low creeping plants.

It is propagated from seed, which is best sown immediately after ripening, either directly *in situ* or in a flower-bed. It is also essential to propagate varieties vegetatively, by division, in spring. It should be planted at intervals of 30—40 cms (12—16 ins).

*Eryngium bourgatii*

128

# *Gypsophila*

Caryophyllaceae
The Pink Family

50—100 cms (1½—3 ft); VI—VII

*Gypsophila paniculata* when fully grown forms large spreading bushes up to over 1 metre (3 ft) high and of similar width. It has profusely branched, thin, jointed stalks with narrow leaves set in pairs, similar to those of Carnations. The wiry sprays of innumerable white or pink florets create a cloud-like effect. The original species has very tiny white flowers, but its varieties have larger flowers and some pink forms have also been developed.

*G. paniculata* var. *flore-pleno* has small, white, double flowers, 60—80 cms (2—2½ ft) high. *G. p.* 'Bristol Fairy' is a variety which also has white double flowers but larger in size; it grows 100—120 cms (3—4 ft) high. *G. p.* 'Flamingo' has light pink, double flowers, with a bushy growth of about 100—120 cms (3—4 ft) in height. *G. p.* 'Rosenschleier' is a low-growing variety, 30—50 cms (1—1½ ft) high, with pink, double flowers, suitable for rockeriers and garden walls. It is propagated by cuttings in May and June.

These plants can withstand excessive dryness, because they have strong roots which penetrate deeply. As they fade and the flowers dry up, the plant is still attractive and will last at least a month before the stalks and leaves turn to autumn rust. It is then necessary to cut the bush to ground level.

*Gypsophila* is useful as a solitary on the lawn or as a contrast in a mosaic of carpeting plants and grasses. It is very suitable for cutting and it is used in bouquets to obtain a lighter effect.

The original species is propagated from seed. The best distance for planting is 70—80 cms (2¼—2½ ft).

*Gypsophila paniculata*

# *Helianthemum*

SUN ROSE

15—25 cms (6—10 ins); VI—VII

Cistaceae

The Rock Rose Family

Sun Roses are used as low-growing perennials, although they are in fact trailing bushy shrubs which bear a profusion of shining, brightly-coloured flowers. The blossoms are single or double. The delicate, branching stems are covered with evergreen oval leaves. The most significant for garden purposes are varieties of *Helianthemum nummularium* which have been developed by cross-breeding various species and whose blossoms provide a pleasing and beautiful decoration for sunny places in the garden. The following are good varieties:

*H. n.* 'Ben Lui' is a large-flowered and dark red Sun Rose, while *H. n.* 'Butter and Eggs' is orange with salmon-tinted, double flowers; *H. n.* 'Cerise Queen' is pink-red with double flowers; *H. n.* 'Citronella' is a single lemon-yellow form and *H. n.* 'Gelbe Perle' is yellow and double flowered.

Sun Roses love calcareous, well-drained soil. They cannot stand damp places and must have a warm and sunny location. In favourable conditions Sun Roses last in one position for many years. They are very well adapted to rockeries in sunny places, garden walls, borders and as low growths in informal beds.

Propagation is by cuttings either in early spring or at the end of August under glass. They should be planted out in spring, 30 cms (12 ins) apart; the species can also be grown from seed. If the bushes are thin and straggly, it is useful to trim them down occasionally to make them thicker; the best time to do this is from May to June.

*Helianthemum hybridum*

# *Lychnis chalcedonica*

JERUSALEM CROSS,
CAMPION

80—100 cms (2½—3 ft); VI—VII

Silenaceae

The Pink Family

This plant is a favourite, especially in established gardens. It comes from the Ukraine and Siberia. It forms upright bushes of unbranched stalks with oval leaves set in pairs; the whole plant is covered with rough hair. In the flowering season each stalk terminates in a thick, round head consisting of small, brilliant red flowers. Apart from the Oriental Poppy, very few other perennials have this intense scarlet colour.

The plant is quite undemanding and grows well in any average garden soil in a sunny position. It will also tolerate slight shade. It is best planted in mixed perennial borders, where the plant's dazzling colour makes it prominent, and it stands out well in association with Ox-eye Daisies and blue Delphiniums. It is also a good plant for cutting.

It is easily propagated by division in spring or in autumn. It can also be grown from seed in spring. The seeds germinate very well and quickly and by autumn the young plants are ready to be planted out, at intervals of 40—60 cms (16—24 ins).

*Lychnis chalcedonica*

# *Heuchera*

CORAL BELLS

30—60 cms (1—2 ft); VI—VII

Saxifragaceae

The Saxifrage Family

This is a low-growing perennial with a basal rosette of heart-shaped leaves with serrated edges. The airy sprays of tiny bell-shaped flowers grow on wiry stems about 30—60 cms (1—2 ft) long. This delicate, vividly coloured flower is very popular and its use is widespread. Several species are cultivated, but particularly the following:

*Heuchera brizoides* 'Gracillima' is a form with small racemes of pink biossoms 50 cms (20 ins) high; *H. sanguinea* 'Splendens' has lustrous coral-red flowers, 40 cms (16 ins) high. Many varieties exist in other colours ranging from white and pink to a vivid red.

It thrives best in a well-drained, calcareous soil, which is not too heavy and to which a little sand and peat have been added. If it has sufficient moisture, it can be left in the sun. It will also tolerate half-shade.

It is at home in rockeries, or in the front of borders in association with other smaller perennials.

It is propagated by division in spring. Some species, such as *H. sanguinea*, can also be grown from seed. The fine seed germinates quickly and successfully. It should be planted out at intervals of 30 cms (12 ins).

*Heuchera sanguinea* 'Splendens'

136

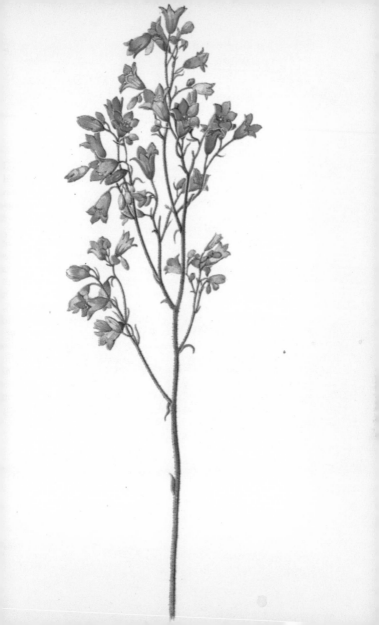

# *Chrysanthemum roseum* *(Pyrethrum roseum)*

Compositae

PYRETHRUM

The Daisy Family

50—80 cms (1½—2½ ft); VI—VII

Pyrethrum flowers are similar to Ox-eye Daisies, but grow in various shades of pink and red as well as white, and they can be either single or double. Delicate pinnate, deep green leaves make up the basal tuft, from which several, usually unbranched, stalks 50—70 cms (1½—2¼ ft) high spring in the flowering season, bearing the flowers. The original species comes from the mountain meadows of the Caucasus. The plant has been much improved and its varieties are outstanding not only because of their large flowers, but also because of their beautiful vibrant colours.

*Ch. r.* 'Laurin' has a profusion of single, salmon-pink flowers, and is low-growing. It measures only 30 cms (1 ft). *Ch. r.* 'Kelway's Glorious' is a variety with dark red, single flowers, also 30 cms (1 ft) high. *Ch. r.* 'Eileen May Robinson' has large, single, pure pink flowers, 80 cms (2½ ft) tall. *Ch. r.* 'Regent' is its red counterpart. *Ch. r.* 'Yvonne Cayeux' has a double white flower with a creamy centre; it grows to a height of about 70 cms (2¼ ft) and is suitable for cutting.

Pyrethrum needs a sunny location and rich, porous soil. It must have sufficient moisture in spring.

It is a very suitable flower for cutting and its blossoms last a long time. It is usually planted in mixed borders. Low-growing varieties are even suitable for edgings and formal bedding.

Pyrethrum is propagated easily by division after flowering or from seed. It should be planted at intervals of 40 cms (16 ins).

*Chrysanthemum roseum*

# *Incarvillea*

30—80 cms (1—2½ ft); VI—VII

This is a very beautiful and interesting perennial coming from China and until recently little known. It has a large, branched, turnip-like root and bold, dark green foliage. The flowers are relatively large, trumpet-shaped and deep pink. They are clustered in twos to tens on a strong stalk.

*Incarvillea grandiflora* is only about 25—30 cms (10—12 ins) high; the lower leaves are pinnate and slightly indented, and the large, pink flowers up to 8 cms (3½ ins) long, grow in ones or twos on a short stalk. It flowers at the end of May and in June. *I. grandiflora* var. *brevipes* has wider, less subdivided leaves and the stalks carry up to five large, vibrant pink blossoms. *I. g.* 'Bess Pink' is a variety only 20 cms (8 ins) tall. Its buds are initially salmon-pink, but later the blossoms turn to lilac-pink. *I. delavayi* is another larger species of *Incarvillea*; its strong stems 70—80 cms (2¼—2½ ft) high bearing clusters of ten to fifteen pink flowers rise from the basal rosette of large, pinnate leaves 30—40 cms (12—16 ins) long.

*Incarvillea* grows best in a nourishing, deep, well-drained loam in a slightly shady position, but not in full shade. Good drainage is important. It cannot stand winter dampness, and in any case should be protected from severe frosts.

It is a very ornamental plant, and therefore shows to best advantage in isolation or in small groups among low carpeting plants. The smaller varieties are useful in the rockery.

It is propagated mainly from seed, which germinates well and quickly. It should be planted at intervals of 30—50 cms (12—20 ins).

*Incarvillea grandiflora*

# *Thalictrum*

MEADOW RUE

80—150 cms (2½—5 ft); V—VII

Ranunculaceae
The Buttercup Family

The genus *Thalictrum* is spread throughout the temperate and sub-tropical zones of the world and takes many forms. Some of them are cultivated in gardens as pleasing and interesting perennials. *Thalictrum aquilegifolium* is the most handsome of these; it is a perennial with finely divided round leaves, similar to those of Columbines. It flowers from mid-May to June. The blossoms are very attractive and unusual. The flowers themselves measure only about 15 mm (½ in.) and are inconspicuous and soon drop. It is then that the stamens with their whitish or lilac-coloured filaments assume importance. These stamens are so distinctive that they are the chief attraction and, seemingly, the only organs of the flower. The whole plant is very decorative.

Meadow Rue is not a demanding plant, although dry conditions do not do it any good. Moist soil in half-shade is the most suitable environment. It can endure a sunny position if, at the same time, it has sufficient moisture.

It is suitable for mixed borders or individual groups in large gardens and parks. It is propagated either by division or from seed. When sown in spring, the plants mature by autumn.

The extremely attractive and interesting species, *T. diptero-carpum*, is also worth mentioning. It originated in western China and has only recently been introduced into our gardens. The leaves are similar to the former plant, but thinner, and blossoms are suspended on thread-like stems in tall airy panicles. The long, spiky petals do not fall; they are pink to purple and in flower from July to September. The height is 100—150 cms (3—5 ft).

*Thalictrum aquilegifolium*

142

## *Astilbe*

FALSE GOAT'S BEARD

45—100 cms (1½—3 ft); VI—VIII

Saxifragaceae

The Saxifrage Family

There is no more beautiful perennial for moist and half-shady places than False Goat's Beard. It has vigorous, bushy, rather fern-like foliage, from which the flowers stand out beautifully. And when they come into bloom in the second half of summer, it is difficult to imagine a more picturesque view. Tall plumes of minute fluffy flowers glisten in every shade of white, cream, light pink, carmine and salmon-pink, through the most varied shades of red to purple.

There are many wild species which used to come from China and Japan, but they have not been found in gardens for a long time. European growers have cultivated many beautiful varieties. *Astilbe arendsii* 'Amethyst' has large full pinky-purple racemes of blossom; *A. a.* 'Burgkristal' is snow-white; *A. a.* 'Cattleya' grows strongly and is cattleya or lilac-pink; *A. a.* 'Fanal' is garnet-red; *A. a.* 'Feuer' has flashing red racemes.

False Goat's Beard needs a humous, moist soil with a rather acid reaction. If it has plenty of moisture it can be left in the sun, but it is better in partial shade. It does not need much attention. It lives in one spot for many years and is satisfied with the occasional addition of a good non-alkaline compost.

Its use is very varied. It is suited to mixed borders and the wild garden. It is particularly beautiful if grown as a collection of individual varieties, well blended in colour. It is propagated very easily by division, best of all in spring. It should be planted at intervals of 40 cms (16 ins).

*Astilbe arendsii*

144

## *Centaurea*

KNAPWEED

30—120 cms (1—4 ft); VI—VIII

Compositae

The Daisy Family

The name 'Knapweed' usually calls to mind the blue meadow variety, but as far as perennial Knapweeds are concerned, blue is not the only colour by any means. There are also red, pink, yellow and white forms, some of which are very small, while others are more than 120 cms (4 ft) high. Only a few of the most beautiful and most interesting from the range which can be cultivated as perennials have been selected here.

*Centaurea dealbata* 'Steenbergii' forms large clumps of stalks bearing large purple-red, cornflower-like blossoms with lighter centres. The leaves are pinnately compound, the top ones toothed and grey-green, felt-like on the underside. It flowers in June to July and the flowering plant is 60—80 cms (2—2½ ft) high. It stands out beautifully in mixed borders and natural groups. It is also suitable for cutting. It should be planted in sunny, rather dry places at intervals of 40 cms (16 ins).

*C. macrocephala* is more similar in its appearance to a large yellow thistle than to Knapweed. It forms bushes up to 120 cms (4 ft) high with a dense foliage of toothed leaves. Each stalk carries one large yellow blossom. It flowers from July to August. It is a plant for large gardens and stands out well in informal plantings. It can also be used for cutting. It should be planted at intervals of 60—80 cms (2—2½ ft).

*C. montana* is a shorter species, only 30—50 cms (1—1½ ft) tall, very reminiscent of the wild Knapweed. It forms richly foliated bushes with blue, pink or white flowers, which grow just above the leaves. It flowers from early June to July. It needs soil which keeps moist but is not too nourishing. The distance between plants should be 35 cms (14 ins).

All Knapweeds can be propagated by division or from seed.

*Centaurea dealbata* 'Steenbergii'

146

# *Erigeron*

FLEABANE

40—80 cms (1¼—2½ ft); VI—VIII

Compositae

The Daisy Family

Fleabanes are very similar to the autumn perennials, Michaelmas Daisies, but they have narrower petals, arranged in several rows. There are many species spread all over the world but the most important is *Erigeron speciosus*, from North America. A number of varieties have been bred which are of uncertain origin but known by the name of *E. hybridus*.

*E. h.* 'Darkest of All' has deep violet biossoms, with a golden eye and is 60 cms (2 ft) high. *E. h.* 'Foersters Liebling' is semi-double, pinky-red or yellow; it flowers for a long time and is very useful for cutting; the height is 60 cms (2 ft). *E. h.* 'Lilace' has large, semi-double blossoms, dark lilac in colour and is 70 cms (2¼ ft) high. *E. h.* 'Mrs F. H. Beale' is an early cobalt-blue variety, 30—40 cms (1—1¼ ft) high and suitable for groups. *E. h.* 'Prosperity' has double dark blue blossoms, suitable for cutting and is 60 cms (2 ft) high. *E. h.* 'Rose Triumph' is a variety with large, fully double, clear pink blossoms suitable for cutting; the height is 60 cms (2 ft). *E. h.* 'Violetta' is semi-double, dark purple and 60 cms (2 ft) high. *E. h.* 'Quakeress' has white flowers turning to pink; it is an early variety and is 60 cms (2 ft) high.

Fleabanes grow in any good garden soil with plenty of lime and in a sunny place. Their role is a versatile one: they can be used in flower borders, informal groups and above all for cutting. The cut blossoms keep in a vase up to ten days and even longer.

It is easily propagated by division, best of all early in spring. If the plants are to flower profusely all the time, it is necessary to divide and transplant them every other year. They should be planted at intervals of 40 cms (16 ins).

*Erigeron hybridus* 'Lilace'

## *Hosta (Funkia)*

PLANTAIN LILY

30—80 cms (1—2½ ft); VI—VIII

Liliaceae

The Lily Family

Until recently, this popular perennial, originating in eastern Asia used to be known under the name *Funkia*. It has few flowers, its importance lying mainly in its beautiful foliage, which is particularly long-lasting when grown in half-shady and shady places.

It forms thick clumps of large, wide lanceolate, oval or heart-shaped leaves with a distinctive venation; in some species they are green, in others variegated.

The thin stalks carry a cluster of bell-shaped, slightly drooping flowers with a long, tubular perianth in white, lilac or purple.

The plant dies off in autumn, buds quite late in spring and is in full leaf in June.

*Hosta glauca (H. sieboldiana)* is 40—60 cms (1¼—2 ft) high, and has grey-green leaves with a clearly defined venation. It is one of the most beautiful, leafy, garden perennials and has several important varieties. *H. glauca* var. *gigantea* is the largest. It has steel-blue leaves and its flowers grow to a height of 80 cms (2½ ft). *H. coerulea* is 30—50 cms (1—1½ ft) tall with dark green leaves. Its purple flowers grow well above the leaves. Some varieties have variegated foliage.

Plantain Lilies thrive best in the sun in a nourishing, adequately moist garden soil, but they grow well even in half-shade and shade. They are suitable for individual groups, borders and for growing around pools.

They are easily propagated by dividing the clumps. The species can even be grown from seed, which should be sown immediately after ripening. They should be planted 40 cms (16 ins) apart.

*Hosta sieboldiana*

## *Lathyrus*

PERENNIAL
or EVERLASTING PEA
100—200 cms (3—6 ft); VI—VIII

Leguminosae
The Pea Family

Apart from the well-known annual Sweet Pea, a perennial —
*Lathyrus latifolius* — is also planted. It is, perhaps, not so well known
as some perennials, but its characteristics have earned it a place in
many gardens.

The plants throw out runners 2 metres (6 ft) long with grey-
green, pinnate leaves; the flowers grow in clusters of up to sixteen
blossoms at the end of short, stiff stems and are white, pink and
reddish-pink. In contrast to the annual Sweet Pea, this perennial
species does not smell sweetly.

The plant is very hardy, it grows to a fair size, and produces
a number of beautiful blossoms without attention every year. The
fleshy, branched roots penetrate to a considerable depth and so
ensure a perfect water supply for the plant even in periods of acute
drought.

It is well suited to covering fences, pergolas, patios, etc., and
also as a growth for barren slopes, where other plants will not grow.
It spreads well and it can stand acute drought and scorching heat.
During hot weather, its leaves shade the nearby soil effectively.
It is also suitable for cutting. The flowers are as long-lasting and
decorative as those of the annual Sweet Pea.

In effect it is propagated only from seed. When sown in spring
and transplanted into flower-pots, the plants are ready to be
planted out by the end of summer. They should be planted at
intervals of 60—100 cms (2—3 ft).

*Lathyrus latifolius*

# *Linum*

FLAX

30—70 cms (1—2¼ ft); VI—VIII

Linaceae

The Flax Family

Flax is a plant of ancient lineage, grown for its firm threads. However some perennial types are cultivated for decoration.

*Linum flavum* var. *compactum* originated in the Orient. It forms low-growing compact bushes, 25—35 cms (10—14 ins) high. Its golden-yellow, flat, five-petalled blossoms are up to 2 cms (¾ in.) in diameter. Its ashy-green, lance-shaped leaves are quite large and last throughout winter. It flowers from mid-July and nearly all summer. It is suitable for rockeries, borders and wild gardens. It thrives best in light half-shade, but it can also stand full sun.

Another species, *L. perenne* forms thick bushes 50—70 cms (1½—2¼ ft) tall, with narrow, light green leaves. It bears thin clusters of azure-blue blossoms, up to 3 cms (1¼ ins) in diameter. *L. narbonense* is similar to the former, but its leaves are almost evergreen. The large blossoms are sky blue with a network of darker blue. *L. n.* 'Heavenly Blue' and *L. n.* 'Six Hills' are two attractive varieties, which have large blossoms in flower over a long period.

Both latter types grow well in a warm, sunny place, in calcareous and well-drained soil. They can even endure dryness.

They are most useful in small groups among low grasses and with perennials in larger rockeries or mixed groups.

They are easily propagated from seed; only such species as *L. narbonense* must be divided. They should be planted at intervals of 30—40 cms (12—16 ins).

*Linum flavum* var. *compactum*

# *Thymus*

THYME

2—5 cms ($\frac{3}{4}$—2 ins); VI—VIII

This is a creeping, pungently aromatic plant, flowering in variou colours. *Thymus serpyllum*, the original type of Thyme, is wide spread throughout Europe and Asia, where it can be found up t 4,000 metres (12,000 ft) above sea level; it is a very good garde plant. It forms thick mats of small, slightly hairy, dark gree leaves. The flowers are very small and arranged in termina clusters; the colours range from white and pink to red.

Thymes love sunny positions, sandy, rather poor soil an dryness. If the soil is too nourishing and moist, they grow too muc and usually soon die away. Otherwise they are very hardy an undemanding plants. They are very well suited to rockeries, dr walls and in between stepping stones. They do not mind bein walked on so can even be used as a substitute for a lawn in dr sunny places. Thyme is an invaluable creeper for covering up th empty spaces left by bulbous flowers when they have died down However in rockeries care must be taken that its invasive growt does not choke more delicate plants. Thymes are one of the mos valuable carpeting plants for natural groups, especially in associa tion with grasses *(Festuca, Avena)*, Stonecrops, Bellflower *(Campa nula pusilla)*, Speedwell *(Veronica rupestris)*, etc.

It is propagated very easily by division or cuttings which shoul be planted at intervals of 20 cms (8 ins).

*Thymus serpyllu*

156

## *Coreopsis*

TICKSEED

40—80 cms (1¼—2½ ft); VI—IX

Compositae

The Daisy Family

Tickseeds are quite tall, profusely flowering perennials which usually have golden-yellow blossoms. Of the perennial varieties suitable for the garden, *Coreopsis grandiflora* should be mentioned, as this is the most frequently cultivated. The plant is about 80 cm (2½ ft) high, slender and irregularly branched with three- to five lobed leaves. The large blossoms — up to 9 cms (4 ins) in diameter — are set individually on long stalks and are golden-yellow. They open from July to August and flower continuously. After they fade away, it is necessary to trim the plant so that it does not become weak. The flowers are quite long lasting and therefore they are primarily suitable for cutting, but also for mixed borders. This species is not always a perennial.

*C. verticillata* is a species which forms dense low bushes, 40—60 cms (1¼—2 ft) high, with finely divided leaves. The pale yellow blossoms are much smaller than those of the former species — about 4 cms (1¾ ins) in diameter — but the flowering period is longer. It flowers from June until autumn. *C. grandiflora* is a variety with larger blossoms, which preserves the good characteristics of the original species. It is a very valuable perennial for mixed borders and for informal groups. It keeps for years in one position and flowers profusely every year without much attention.

Neither species has special requirements as to soil. The average well-drained garden soils are suitable for them, but they do not like winter dampness. The location should be in full sunshine.

*C. verticillata* is propagated by division; *C. grandiflora* from seed. They should be planted at intervals of 40 cms (16 ins).

*Coreopsis grandiflora*

158

## *Heliopsis*

Compositae

ORANGE SUNFLOWER

The Daisy Family

80—120 cms (2½—4 ft); VI—IX

Of several species, all of which come from North America, *Heliopsis scabra* is the one usually cultivated in gardens. It forms thick clumps of deep green, oval leaves with serrated edges. The blossoms are shaped like small Sunflowers and are golden-yellow. A number of single and semi-double varieties are cultivated from the basic species.

*H. scabra* 'Patula' has large semi-double flowers up to 10 cms (4 ins) across, and is about 100 cms (3 ft) tall. It flowers continuously from June to September. It can be propagated by seed. Another variety *H. s.* 'Summer Sun' is taller and has orange-yellow blossoms with delicately radiating petals. Finally *H. s.* 'Zinnia' has double blossoms, reminiscent in shape of dahlia-flowered zinnias. Its height is 80 cms (2½ ft).

*Heliopsis* grows well in any average garden soil, as long as it is not too dry in summer. However in winter damp conditions are harmful. The most suitable position is in full sunshine, although it can temporarily survive in shade.

*Heliopsis* is suitable for flower borders, providing patches of rich golden-yellow. But it must be borne in mind that these are tall plants and so they should be set towards the back. They are also suitable for cutting, especially *H. scabra* 'Patula', whose flowers keep in a vase some eight to ten days.

It is easily propagated by division or by taking cuttings in spring. *H. scabra* 'Patula' can also be sown.

The plants can live for years in one place and flower inexhaustibly every year. It is useful to feed them occasionally with a good compost or manure. They should be planted at intervals of 60 cms (2 ft).

*Heliopsis scabra* 'Patula'

# *Scabiosa*
SCABIOUS
50—80 cms (1½—2½ft;) VI—IX

Dipsacaceae
The Teasel Family

*Scabiosa caucasica*, originating in the Caucasus, is the most suitable for gardens of the many perennial species of Scabious. The basal leaves are elongate, often pinnate, and divided into narrow segments. The blossoms are up to 8 cms (3 ins) in diameter; those of this garden species are light blue, but numerous varieties have been developed with various shades of blue, purple and white flowers.

*Scabiosa caucasica* 'Blauer Atlas' is a deep purple-blue, large-flowered Scabious, about 80 cms (2½ ft) high. *S. c.* 'Chalenger' is a variety 70 cms (2¼ ft) tall with large deep blue blossoms on stiff stems. *S. c.* 'Oliver Greaves' has a profusion of light purple blossoms. It is a popular variety for cutting, and is 80 cms (2½ ft) high. *S. c.* 'Doreen' is a very early variety with striking brilliant blue blossoms, 70 cms (2¼ ft) high. *S. c.* 'Miss Willmott' has notably large, pure white flowers produced in profusion. It is about 80 cms (2½ ft) high. *S. c.* 'Perfecta' is clear blue and 80 cms (2½ ft) high, while *S. c.* 'Souter's Violet' has large, dark purple-blue flowers and is about 60 cms (2 ft) high.

Scabious needs sun and a warm, dry position with a light, well-drained soil. It cannot stand too much moisture, especially in winter. Depending on the quality of the soil, it is useful to divide and transplant the plant every third or fifth year.

It has a very long flowering season and the cut blossoms are quite long-lived; it is, therefore, a valuable flower for cutting. Otherwise it is suitable for borders and mixed groups.

It is propagated from seed in spring. Yet it is also necessary to propagate some varieties vegetatively by division in spring. It should be planted at intervals of 40 cms (16 ins).

*Scabiosa caucasica*

# *Gaillardia*

BLANKET FLOWER

30—80 cms (1—2½ ft); VI—X

Compositae

The Daisy Family

Blanket Flowers are very rewarding and beautiful perennials for summer time. Their brilliant daisy-like blossoms begin to open in June. They are in full flower by July, and continue, though less profusely, until the end of September and often until October. The leaves are grey-green, hairy and partly indented, and the flower stalks are similarly hairy.

Many varieties have been cultivated, which in recent gardening catalogues are listed as having arisen from *Gaillardia aristata*. *G. a.* 'Burgundy' is a variety which has single-colour, wine-red blossoms, 60—70 cms (2—2¼ ft) high. *G. a.* 'Ipswich Beauty' is red banded with yellow, large-flowered and 70 cms (2¼ ft) high. *G. a.* 'Copper Beauty' is red-yellow, small, compact and 25—30 cms (9 ins—1 ft) high, and the variety *G. a.* 'Firebrand' is a single-colour, orange-bronze, about 70 cms (2¼ ft) high.

The Blanket Flower is suitable for light, well-drained soils, in a warm, sunny place. In these conditions it lasts for several years; otherwise it is counted as a biennial. It is not suited to damp soils or shade. Taller varieties tend to grow too tall if the soil is too nourishing and flop about and even lie down flat. In spite of their short life, Blanket Flowers are popular in gardens because of their rich colouring and long flowering period.

They are useful in borders and are excellent for cutting. The small, compact varieties are suitable for larger rockeries and for edging formal flower-beds.

It is usually propagated from seed, which germinates quickly and very well. It should be planted at intervals of 40 cms (16 ins).

*Gaillardia aristata*

## *Oenothera*

EVENING
PRIMROSE

20—30 cms (8—12 ins); VI—X

Onagraceae
The Willow-herb Family

The lesser *Oenothera missouriensis* is the most important of all
Evening Primroses. It comes from the high plains of California,
where it grows in dry, barren places in calcareous soil. That is why
it is so undemanding and vigorous in average garden conditions.
The drooping stalks are densely foliated with narrow leaves,
similar to those of a willow or peach tree. The flowers are sulphur-
yellow, wide open, up to 15 cms (6 ins) in diameter; they open
continuously in great numbers, so that from the end of June until
October the plant is almost ceaselessly in flower, but its main
flowering season is July to August.

It grows well in nearly any soil, but a dry and sunny place is
preferable. The roots are fleshy and reach quite deep down.

Evening Primrose is suitable for larger rockeries, where it lasts
a very long time and is of particular value as it flowers throughout
the summer when other rock flowers are scarce. However it is
essential to remember its vigorous, trailing growth, which can
choke more delicate rockery plants if it is planted too close.
Evening Primrose looks well in group plantings, where it forms
a picturesque setting for some of the taller perennials that flower
in summer. It must be borne in mind, however, that Evening
Primrose buds as late as May, so that until then the bed will be
empty. It can, therefore, be combined very effectively with some
of the spring bulbous flowers, which flower in spring and shrivel
up when Evening Primrose begins to grow.

It is propagated from seed, which germinates easily and when
sown in spring the seedlings are ready to be planted out in autumn.
They should be planted at intervals of 40—60 cms (16—24 ins).

*Oenothera missouriensis*

166

# *Chrysanthemum* Compositae
# *leucanthemum maximum*
OX-EYE DAISY                                       The Daisy Family
60—100 cms (2—3 ft); VII

Ox-eye Daisy is a well-known meadow flower, which in its larger-flowered forms is cultivated in many gardens. Garden Ox-eye Daisies developed mainly by crossbreeding three species: *Chrysanthemum leucanthemum*, *Ch. maximum* and *Ch. latifolium*. *Ch. leucanthemum* is a well-known spring meadow Ox-eye Daisy; *Ch. maximum* and *Ch. latifolium* are large-flowered Ox-eye Daisies. Excellent varieties have been developed from them, of which only a few are mentioned here. *Ch. leucanthemum maximum* 'Beethoven' has large blossoms on strong stalks and is about 80 cms (2½ ft) high. The variety *Ch. l. m.* 'Mayfield Giant' has huge blossoms up to 20 cms (8 ins) in diameter, *Ch. l. m.* 'Moonlight' has stiff stalks which do not need staking, and double, beautifully shaped blossoms; it is 60 cms (2 ft) high. *Ch. l. m.* 'Wirral Supreme' has double flowers, up to 10 cms (4 ins) in diameter and is 80 cms (2½ ft) high.

Ox-eye Daisies' chief claim to popularity is their excellence as cut flowers. The blossoms are very long-lived, especially the semi-double and double varieties. The taller varieties, however, often flop about and sometimes fall to the ground. Smaller varieties are firmer, and therefore suitable for formal beds as well as freely designed groups.

The soil should be nourishing, well drained and even heavy if it is sufficiently moist. The large-flowered varieties are more demanding than the small-flowered ones. A sunny position is important.

Ox-eye Daisies are not long-lasting perennials. If they are left in one place for several years, they often do not survive the winter. It is therefore necessary to divide and transplant the clumps in early autumn every or every other year.

They are propagated mainly by division. They should be planted at intervals of 40—60 cms (16—24 ins).

*Chrysanthemum leucanthemum maximum*

# *Verbascum*

MULLEIN

150—200 cms (5—6½ ft); VII

Scrophulariaceae
The Foxglove Family

Mulleins are widespread in the wild state and are found above all on stony, dry, even parched, slopes, seemingly unaffected by these barren conditions.

The majority of Mulleins are biennials. They form large rosettes of grey, spear-shaped leaves in the first year from which, in the second year, rises a strong stalk like a candlestick bearing numbers of small, shallow, five-petalled flowers.

*Verbascum olympicum* is one of the largest and most beautiful. It comes from Asia Minor. In the flowering season it grows into a huge plant, more than 2 metres (6½ ft) high. Its strong stalk is branched and forms large spikes of yellow blossoms. If the fading flowerheads are removed in time, it lasts a third year. It seeds itself very easily.

Mullein is most useful as a focal point in a set-piece of three to five plants, either in the lawn or in grassed areas in association with creeping plants.

It grows best in a well-drained, dry, rather calcareous soil. Of necessity it requires a sunny place and does not mind a very dry position. It grows even better in a richer soil.

It is easily propagated from seed, which is very fine and germinates well, best of all at the end of May to June. When the young plants have developed good root systems — usually best in August — they can be planted out. If Mulleins are required year after year in the same place, it is useful to have a supply of young plants ready and transplant them each year to the chosen position. They should be planted 1 metre (3 ft) apart.

*Verbascum olympicum*

# *Echinops*

GLOBE THISTLE

100—150 cms (3—5 ft); VII—VIII

Composita

The Daisy Family

This is an interesting plant, rather like a thistle, with finely divided, prickly leaves and an attractive, blue globular flowerhead

*Echinops ritro*, particularly, is cultivated in our gardens; in the wild, it grows freely from south-eastern Europe to the Altai mountains. Several varieties have been developed with especially fine flowerheads. *E. r.* 'Blue Globe' is a variety with a large, dark blue inflorescence with a silvery sheen and is 120 cms (4 ft) high. The variety *E. r.* 'Taplow Blue' has beautiful, steel-blue blossoms and is 120 cms (4 ft) high.

The Globe Thistle is not particular as to growing conditions. Its main requirements are sunshine and a rather dry, light and poor soil. It grows freely and soon droops when planted in a soil which is too rich.

It is suitable for colourful formal flower-beds and borders, and also wild gardens. It is also suitable for cutting.

The Globe Thistle can remain for many years in one place; it does not mind the encroachment of grass or other plants as its roots reach to a considerable depth. It does not need any attention.

It is propagated from seed, and often seeds itself. However the varieties must be propagated vegetatively, by division of roots or root cuttings taken in early spring. It should be planted at intervals of 60 cms (2 ft).

*Echinops ritro*

# *Helenium*

SNEEZEWEED

70—150 cms (2¼—5 ft); VII—VIII

Compositae
The Daisy Family

Sneezeweeds are as beautiful and give as much pleasure as Cone-flowers; they bloom in late summer with a profusion of yellow and red shading to brown daisy-like flowers with striking globular central disks. The most valuable are hybrids, of which the following are among the best.

*Helenium hybridum* 'Bruno' is a warm mahogany-red, medium early variety about 100 cms (3 ft) high. *H. h.* 'Butterpat' is a deep yellow, medium early variety of about the same height; *H. h.* 'Crimson Beauty' is copper-red with a dark centre; it is an early variety and is 60 cms (2 ft) high. *H. h.* 'Flammenrad' has golden-yellow blossoms with red-brown flecks, is medium early and 150 cms (5 ft) high. *H. h.* 'Goldlackzwerg' is bronze-red with yellow edges, medium early, and 80 cms (2½ ft) high. *H. h.* 'Kanaria' has golden flowers with a light centre, and grows to a height of 120 cms (4 ft). *H. h.* 'Karneol' is copper-red with a brown centre, medium early and 100 cms (3 ft) high; *H. h* 'Little Red Riding Hood' is a beautiful, shorter variety, with red-brown flowers growing to a height of 80 cms (2½ ft). *H. h.* 'Wal-traud' has large, golden-brown, yellow-toned flowers; it is early and grows 100 cms (3 ft) high. *H. h.* 'Morheim Beauty' has glowing bronze-red flowers 100 cms (3 ft) high and is the most popular variety in Britain.

Sneezeweeds require a soil rich in humus, adequately moist but not too wet. They thrive only in a sunny position; occasional feeding in spring is good for them. Dead flowers should be removed to prevent the plants from becoming weak.

Sneezeweeds are mainly used in mixed borders. They also stand out beautifully in large groups in front of dark conifers, and are very suitable for cutting.

They are very easily propagated by dividing the roots in spring. They should be planted 50 cms (20 ins) apart.

*Helenium hybridum*

# *Lavandula*

LAVENDER
30—40 cms (1—1¼ ft); VII—VIII

Labiatae
The Mint Family

Lavender is a very well-known flower. It is often cultivated in gardens, and is popular for the colour of its blossoms and particularly for its sweet scent. It is, in fact, a small shrub. In some countries it is cultivated in vast areas as the raw material for the production of lavender oil, which is used in medicine, in the manufacture of lacquer for painting china, and as a perfume for scenting eau de cologne, soaps, etc.

The most popular garden variety is *Lavandula officinalis (L. vera)*. It grows wild in the Mediterranean on limestone slopes. It forms densely foliated bushes with tough, narrow, greyish, evergreen leaves. The short spikes of blue blossom on leafless stalks appear in about July. Several varieties have been developed which are notable for the size and colour of their flowers.

Lavender needs full sunshine and a rather dry calcareous soil, which need not be of very good quality. It is a very versatile plant. It can be grown in the border or it can be planted in groups. The effect is outstanding when it is planted among carpets of Thyme or some other creeping perennial. It is also effective in association with certain grasses, especially those of the genus *Festuca*.

It can be used to form low, evergreen hedges round flower-beds and shaped by trimming.

Lavender is propagated either from seed or from cuttings. The young plants are potted, and later transplanted at intervals of 40 cms (16 ins).

*Lavandula officinalis*

176

## *Monarda*
BERGAMOT
80—100 cms (2½—3¼ ft); VII—VIII

Labiatae
The Mint Family

Aromatic Bergamot comes from North America, where it grows in damp places. Of many popular species *Monarda didyma* is especially important for gardeners. It has lanceolate, sharply defined leaves and erect leafy stems crowned by terminal clusters of long, tubular, lipped flowers, which give a rather exotic impression. The whole plant is finely haired and has a unique sweet smell.

From all the varieties the following at least should be mentioned: *Monarda didyma* 'Adam' is cherry-red, 100 cms (3¼ ft) high; *M. d.* 'Blue Stocking' is lilac-blue and taller; *M. d.* 'Cambridge Scarlet' is dark scarlet, 100 cms (3¼ ft) high. The variety *M. d.* 'Melissa' is light pink and 90 cms (3 ft) high and *M. d.* 'Croftway Pink' is a rich rosy-pink and 90 cms (3 ft) high. *M. d.* 'Snow Maiden' is white-flowered and has paler foliage. It is 90 cms (3 ft) high.

Bergamot is not demanding and is a very rewarding perennial, which can last a long time in one place. It grows well in any garden soil, dry or damp, in the sun or mild, half-shade. Older, well-established plants produce a beautiful, colourful effect wherever they are planted. They are suitable for borders as well as for cutting and informal groups, and are much loved by bees.

The easiest methods of propagation are by division and also by cuttings, which root well. They should be planted at intervals of 60 cms (2 ft).

*Monarda didyma* 'Cambridge Scarlet'

## *Phlox*

Polemoniaceae

PHLOX

The Jacob's Ladder Family

50—120 cms (1½—4 ft); VII—VIII

Phlox is a richly flowering perennial and includes many species, of which *Phlox paniculata (P. decussata)* is the most important for gardens; this has been cultivated in a great number of varieties of all colours from white, through every shade of pink to red and purple. The blossoms are of one colour or have variegated eyes or patterns.

Phlox forms clumps of firm stalks foliated with wide lanceolate leaves. The stalks terminate in broad, flat racemes of blossoms. It is possible to count the varieties in hundreds; only a few of the more important are mentioned here.

*P. paniculata* 'Jules Sandeau' is carmine-pink, 50 cms (20 ins) high and *P. p.* 'Mia Ruys' is a pure white, 40 cms (16 ins) high and both belong to the earliest flowering group. *P. p.* 'September Snow' is white with a delicate pink eye, 80—100 cms (2½—3 ft) high, and *P. p.* 'Starfire' is vermilion-red with a dark eye and is 100 cms (3 ft) high. These are both very late varieties.

Phloxes thrive best in a deep, loose, well-drained, nourishing humous soil. They need to be watered during dry periods, especially when full grown. It is useful to feed them in winter by digging in a good compost or peat manure. A sunny position is best, but they grow well even in mild shade, although they then grow taller and flower later. Under good conditions and with systematic feeding they last for many years in one place.

They are used in borders where they make colourful groups. They are less suitable for natural areas or wild gardens.

They are easily propagated by dividing the clumps or by root cuttings in spring. They root well under glass. They should be planted at intervals of 40 cms (16 ins).

*Phlox paniculata*

180

# *Platycodon*

BALLOON FLOWER

40—70 cms (1¼—2¼ ft); VII—VIII

Campanulaceae

The Bellflower Family

The Balloon Flower looks very similar and is related to the Bell-flowers. It comes from eastern Asia. It has fleshy, white, tuberous roots, and thin, upright stems with tough, egg-shaped, lanceolate leaves with finely serrated edges. It has curious purple-blue buds hermetically sealed like balloons which burst into wide five-pointed, star-shaped flowers.

*Platycodon grandiflorum* is the only species of this genus. It is 50—70 cms (1½—2¼ ft) high and has blue flowers, up to 8 cms (3 ins) in diameter. Of its varieties, *P. g.* var. *album* has white flowers with a network of blue veins. P. g. 'Roseum' is a delicate pink variety and *P. g.* 'Mariesii' is a smaller blue variety which flowers profusely.

Balloon Flower is a beautiful late autumn perennial with many possibilities. It is a good plant for the front of borders and wild gardens where it stands out splendidly among growths of grey-leaved creeping plants.

It grows best in a sunny position, but it can also stand light shade. It grows well in any well-drained garden soil, which is not too damp or wet in winter.

It will last in one place for several years. However, older plants often flop; this defect can be prevented by shortening the shoots about 10 cms (4 ins) in June. The plants then become bushier and more compact and flower in greater profusion.

Balloon Flower is propagated mainly from seed. It should be planted at intervals of 30—40 cms (12—16 ins).

*Platycodon grandiflorum*

# *Rodgersia*

Saxifragaceae<br>The Saxifrage Family

60—150 cms (2—5 ft); VII—VIII

Rodgersias are striking plants and their big, beautifully formed leaves are especially ornamental. The majority of species have a bulky rosette of leaves, from which stalks bearing branched racemes of tiny flowers grow at the end of summer. The majority of species come from China and three of these are usually cultivated in gardens.

*Rodgersia tabularis* with large, round leaves held flat on stalks coming from the centre, is the first and most beautiful. Their huge leaves are sometimes up to 80 cms (2½ ft) in diameter. The blossoms are white in a long raceme, which later on arches a little. *R. podophylla* is up to 1 metre (3 ft) high with large, palmate leaves. The blossoms are white in a long branched raceme. The third species is *R. aesculifolia*, which has palmate leaves strongly reminiscent of those of the Horse Chestnut. Its racemes of fine, white blossoms reach over 150 cms (5 ft) in length.

*Rodgersia* grows best in a deep, nourishing, slightly damp humous soil and in half-shade. It will even tolerate total shade.

Its beautiful leaves and habit stand out best when planted as a solitary. Larger groups of Rodgersias are decorative planted beside water, or in shady corners among trees and shrubs. However they do not fit in with ordinary perennials. They require the simplest grouping and setting either on a lawn or among a carpet of low-growing perennials.

It is propagated by division in spring or by root cuttings in autumn in a greenhouse. Propagation from seed is also possible, but it is necessary to isolate the parent plants. It should be planted at intervals of 70—100 cms (2¼—3 ft).

*Rodgersia tabularis*

# *Stachys*

LAMB'S EAR

30—60 cms (1—2 ft); VII—VIII

Labiatae

The Mint Family

Lamb's Ear is a genus which is widespread all over the world. The two most commonly grown species are *Stachys lanata* and *S. grandiflora*. *S. lanata* forms a thick, low growth of elongated oval, thick, silvery felt-like leaves, which are the main feature of this perennial. The flower stalks grow about 30—50 cms (12—20 ins) high and terminate in clusters of small pink blossoms at the leaf axil. The flowers, however, are usually cut away so that they do not detract from the attractive, thick, leafy growth.

*Stachys lanata* needs a dry and sunny location; it easily rots in damp conditions. The soil should be rather light and well drained. It is used on dry walls and in large rockeries, where it does not matter if it spreads freely. It is also excellent planted in groups in a spacious setting or even as a substitute for a lawn. It is easily propagated by division and should be planted at intervals of 30—40 cms (12—15 ins).

*S. grandiflora* is a perennial 30—50 cms (12—20 ins) high, forming bushes of oval heart-shaped leaves with serrated edges. Its flowers consist of heads of lavender-pink blossoms, reminiscent of Lilac.

It requires the same conditions as *S. lanata* and can be planted in half-shade as well as full sun.

It is a very pleasing perennial in formal borders or in isolated groups. It is easily propagated by division. The plants should be 30—40 cms (12—16 ins) apart.

*Stachys lanata*

## *Statice*                    Plumbaginaceae
SEA LAVENDER              The Plumbago Family
40—60 cms (16—24 ins); VII—VIII

Some authors have recently called this genus *Limonium*. It includes annuals and perennials, but all are conditioned to a very dry habitat. The perennial species have a basal rosette of leathery spoon-like leaves and tough, wide-spreading, branching stems thickly clustered with hundreds of minute mauve flowers.

As regards garden decoration, *Statice latifolia* comes into its own. In the wild, it grows freely on the grassy steppes of south-eastern Europe. The plants have strong, deeply penetrating roots. The tongue-like leaves are deep green, elongated and ovate, covered with fine hair. They form a basal rosette and remain green even throughout winter, so that they are a decoration in themselves.

In the summer flowering period the plant forms several profusely branched stalks which bear innumerable tiny light lavender-blue blossoms. Sea Lavender can easily be dried for winter decoration if it is cut just when the flowers are opening and hung in a dark place.

The plants need as much sunshine as possible and well-drained, calcareous soil. They cannot stand wet conditions, particularly in winter.

They should, therefore, be planted on dry walls, sun-baked slopes and any situation where dry conditions limit the choice of plants. They stand out beautifully in isolated groups and in the company of creeping plants and grasses.

It is propagated mainly from seed. When sown in spring, the plants are ready to be planted out in autumn. They live many years, and flower even when choked by grass. They should be planted at intervals of 50—60 cms (20—24 ins).

*Statice latifolia*

188

## *Echinacea*
PURPLE CONEFLOWER
80—100 cms (2½—3 ft); VII—IX

Compositae
The Daisy Family

Until a few years ago this plant was known under the name *Rudbeckia purpurea* and only recently has it been given its own genus. It is quite similar to Coneflowers in the construction of its flowers and leaves, but no Coneflower has such a purple-pink colour or such a large, spike-like central cone.

*Echinacea* comes from North America. Its long, oval leaves and stems are both covered with tough hairs, which makes the whole plant very rough. The blossoms are set individually on firm stalks; they are more than 15 cms (6 ins) in diameter, purple-pink, with a striking, spiky, red-brown cone.

Apart from the species, some other varieties are also cultivated, such as *Echinacea purpurea* 'Abendsonne' which has large, carmine-red blossoms. Another variety is *E. p.* 'The King' which has particularly large, dark red blossoms.

It grows well in normal garden soil and will even tolerate dryness very well, but it requires sunshine all the time.

It is useful as a medium-sized perennial in borders. Its whole appearance is a striking feature in informal groups or among low-growing perennials.

It is propagated very easily either by division of the roots in spring, or from seed, which germinates well. When sown in spring, it is possible to transplant the seedlings at the end of summer at intervals of 50—60 cms (20—24 ins).

*Echinacea purpurea*

190

## Physosegia

OBEDIENT PLANT

60—100 cms (2—3 ft); VII—IX

Labiatae

The Mint Family

*Physostegia* is a pleasing and interesting perennial which forms densely foliated bushes. The stalks are quadrangular in section and the narrow, lanceolate dark green leaves are serrated and set in pairs up the stems.

The individual, two-lipped blossoms are about 20—25 mm ($\frac{3}{4}$—1 in.) long and arranged in thin four-angled spikes more than 20 cms (8 ins) long. The flowers of the majority of varieties are pink, but white forms have also been developed. A curious characteristic of this perennial is the hinged fastening of individual blossoms to the spike, so that it is possible to move them from side to side.

This plant is a native of North America, where it grows in the light, damp, mixed deciduous forests of the warmer eastern regions. The genus has five species, but *Physostegia virginiana* with pink, white and red blossoms is mainly cultivated in gardens.

It thrives best in loose, poor, well-drained soil, but it needs adequate moisture in summer, otherwise it loses its leaves. It does well in either a sunny or a half-shaded position.

It is used in borders as a medium-sized late summer perennial. However it is best presented in wild gardens among a carpet of low-growing perennials. It is also valuable for cutting as the blossoms last a long time and open slowly and continuously until the very last bud.

It is easily propagated by division of the clumps or by cuttings. It is best to plant it in spring, at intervals of 40—50 cms (16—20 ins). It develops its full beauty in the second or third year after planting, and if it has suitable conditions, it lives for many years in one place.

*Physostegia virginiana*

192

# *Sedum*

STONECROP

Height variable; VII—IX

Crassulaceae

The Stonecrop Family

Stonecrops form a very large genus which is found all over the northern hemisphere. These plants are decorative both in their blossoms and in the shape and colour of their leaves; they grow very well in the driest, sunniest places. Some low-growing species are well suited to rockeries and to planting over larger areas. Among these *Sedum cauticolum* blooms in September and October, and has carmine-pink to ruby-red flowers. Another Stonecrop, *S. kamtschaticum*, bears orange-yellow flowers in July and August. It forms low bushes with gay yellow leaves.

*Sedum spectabile* is one of the most robust Stonecrops. It grows in clumps 30—50 cms (12—20 ins) tall. Its blue-grey, succulent leaves are ovate and turn golden-yellow in autumn. The firm stalks terminate in large, flat umbels, composed of fine pink blossoms. It flowers at the end of August and in September. Popular varieties are: *S. s.* 'Brilliant', pinkish-red; *S. s.* 'Carmen', carmine-red, and *S. s.* var. *atropurpureum*, a deep dark red. This Stonecrop can be grown on its own in rockeries and borders, but it is especially effective in groups among creeping plants and grasses.

Sedums grow well in ordinary garden soil in full sun. *S. spectabile* is the only Stonecrop which responds to good soil conditions and occasional feeding. All other Stonecrops must be planted in sandy, rather poor, dry soil, otherwise they lose their characteristic growth and colour.

Propagation of all Stonecrops is very easy by division of the roots or by cuttings. They should be planted 20—40 cms (8—16 ins) apart.

*Sedum spectabile* 'Carmen'

# *Tradescantia*

SPIDERWORT         The Spiderwort Family

50—70 cms (1½—2¼ ft); VII—IX

The North American *Tradescantia virginiana* is particularly suitable for our gardens, with its grass-like foliage and habit. At the top of the stalks, in the axil points of large leaf clusters, dense bunches of buds grow, which open gradually. The blue, purple, pink or white flowers are tripartite with a thick soft down on the outer side of the petals. The individual blossoms are short-lived, which gives rise to another common name 'Flower of a Day', but new buds are constantly produced.

Several varieties have been cultivated, of which the following at least must be listed: *Tradescantia virginiana* 'I. C. Weguellin', azure blue; *T. v.* 'Innocence', pure white; *T. v.* 'Iris', deep blue; *T. v.* 'Leonore', gentian-blue; *T. v.* 'Osprey', white with purple stamens; *T. v.* 'Rubra', shiny red; *T. v.* 'Purewell Giant', carmine-red; *T. v.* 'Valour', reddish-purple; and *T. v.* 'Zwannenburg', a particularly large-flowered variety, is blue.

The plants are very easy to grow; as long as they have plenty of light, they can stand both dry and damp conditions. When the soil is sufficiently moist, they flower ceaselessly and remain green for a long time.

Spiderworts are suitable for borders, natural areas and even for growing beside water. The plants can be left undisturbed for several years and grow appreciably in time.

They are propagated mainly by dividing them in spring before they bud too much. They should be planted either in spring or occasionally in autumn so that they root well before winter. The distance between them should be 30—40 cms (12—16 ins).

*Tradescantia virginiana*

# *Anemone japonica*

Ranunculaceae

JAPANESE ANEMONE · · · · · · · · The Buttercup Family

40—120 cms (16 ins—4 ft); VII—X

Japanese Anemones form a very extensive group of plants. They come from China and Japan and are the real jewels of an autumn garden, when the number of flowers is quickly decreasing. The plants mainly cultivated in gardens are hybrids of *Anemone japonica*, which has been much improved in the shape of its blossoms and beautiful range of colours now available.

The plants have three-lobed, basal leaves with slightly hairy undersides. The large, white, pink or red bowl-shaped blossoms are borne freely on thin, branched stalks. The flowers are single or semi-double and have quite large globular pistils with a number of yellow stamens. *A. japonica* 'Géante de Blanche' is 100 cms (3 ft) tall [VIII—X], cream-white and semi-double; *A. j.* 'Hupehensis Praecox' is 40 cms (16 ins) tall [VIII—X], pink, early and small; *A. j.* 'Profusion' is 60 cms (2 ft) tall [IX—XI] semi-double and dark red.

Japanese Anemones are a garden attraction long after the other flowers have been damaged by the frost. They love half-shade and a light, humous soil, best mixed with peat or leaf mould. They need plenty of moisture, but not in winter. It is useful to cover them with a layer of peat or dry leaves during the autumn.

They can be planted in groups in half shade but should not be too close to the roots of trees or shrubs. They stand out beautifully in association with grasses or conifers. The spacing between plants should be 40 cms (16 ins).

It is propagated by division or by root cuttings. However it is necessary to grow the cuttings under glass.

*Anemone japonica* 'Hupehensis Praecox'

## *Physalis*

CHINESE LANTERN

60—80 cms (2—2½ ft); flowers VII
fruits  VIII—X

Solanaceae
The Potato Family

Chinese Lantern is often cultivated in gardens for its fruits, which look like small orange Chinese paper lanterns. In appearance each seed case is like a closed chalice, which contains the fruit, a red berry of the size of a small cherry.

This plant is very invasive. It has straight stalks with oval, smooth-edged leaves. The flowers are undistinguished and whitish in colour. The fruit is the main decoration and remains until winter, even after the leaves have fallen.

The genus has about 100 species, originating mainly in the tropical and subtropical zones of America. In Europe, the two best-known species cultivated are *Physalis alkekengi*, 50—60 cms (1½—2 ft) high, and *P. franchetii*, 60—80 cms (2—2½ ft) high, whose native land is probably Japan. Both species are similar, but the former is smaller, covered with downy hair and has a bright red berry; the latter is taller, smooth, and has a yellow berry.

Chinese Lanterns thrive best in a well-drained, rich, calcareous, rather dry soil, either in the sun or half-shade. The suitability of its position will be reflected in the height of the plant. In favour-able conditions it will spread like a weed, so it is not advisable to put it too close to plants of weaker growth. In fact these plants are best used in places where they can be left to grow completely on their own. They are very valuable for cutting and can be used when dry as an everlasting decoration in vases.

They are easily propagated by division or by cutting the under-ground runners into 10 cms (4 ins) long pieces and planting them 5 cms (2 ins) deep at intervals of 30 cms (12 ins).

*Physalis franchetii*

200

## *Solidago*
GOLDEN ROD

60—150 cms (2—5 ft); VII—X

Compositae

The Daisy Family

Golden Rod is one of the taller perennials characteristic of late summer. It is especially widespread in North America where there are many species growing wild, and by crossbreeding these the cultivated varieties have been developed. The majority of these form large, upright clumps with thin, woody stalks, densely foliated and terminating in wide, frothy racemes of tiny golden-yellow blossoms. These flowerheads are slightly reminiscent of Mimosa. The individual varieties differ from each other in height and the arrangement of racemes. *Solidago hybrida* 'Golden Shower' is one of the best earlier sorts, very like Mimosa, and is 60—80 cms (2—2½ ft) high. *S. h.* 'Goldtanne' has large golden leaves, is 180 cms (6 ft) high and a very late variety [IX—X], while *S. h.* 'Laurin' is only 50 cms (20 ins) high, but this is a more demanding variety.

Golden Rod grows well in almost any soil, dry or damp, in sunshine or half-shade. It seeds readily and the young plants grow up round it like weeds. Self-seeded plants are not usually of a good quality, and it is therefore advisable to cut off the racemes immediately after flowering. The plants last a long time, but it is advisable, however, to divide the clumps occasionally in order to strengthen them.

The taller varieties can be planted at the back of a mixed border, particularly against a darker background. Smaller varieties can also be used in groups among small perennials. In addition, Golden Rod is very suitable for cutting.

It is easily propagated by division or by cuttings, usually best taken in spring. These should be planted 50—60 cms (20—24 ins) apart.

*Solidago hybrida*

# *Liatris*

BLAZING STAR

60—100 cms (2—3 ft); VIII

Compositae

The Daisy Family

This is a perennial which is both beautiful and also very interesting to grow. Its leaves are long and narrow, rather like grass. It has bulbous tubers similar to those of the saffron crocus, except that they do not shrivel up after flowering. Densely foliated stalks spring up in summer, terminating in spikes of small pink flowers with long petals and prominent stamens.

The genus includes about 30 species, which mostly come from North America and are all quite similar in growth. The pink-flowering variety, *Liatris spicata*, is particularly suitable for garden cultivation. *L. s.* 'Kobold' is a small variant of the species and is about 40 cms (16 ins) tall. Otherwise it is similar in flower and foliage to the former.

The plant thrives best in full sunshine. The soil should be fairly porous and dry, but not sun-baked.

*Liatris* is suitable for formal bedding and borders; it is a striking plant not only during the flowering season, but also, because of its foliage, a long time before that. It is also suitable for cutting, for it lasts quite a long time in water and looks exotic.

It is easily propagated, either by division of the tuber clump, which should be done early in spring, or from seed. The seed germinates well, and when planted in spring will produce plants for autumn which will start flowering the following year.

Plants may be left in one place for five or six years; they should then be divided and replanted. This strengthens them and ensures good development for several years. They should be planted at intervals of 40 cms (16 ins).

*Liatris spicata*

# *Ligularia*

100—120 cms (3—4 ft); VIII

These are handsome plants with large, bold leaves. They form big, bushy growths, which stand out beautifully on the banks of ponds or streams and equally in half-shaded, damp parts of the garden, in front of dark conifers or planted simply as solitary groups on the lawn. They produce several upright stalks with clusters of yellow or orange flowers at the end of summer. The individual species differ in height, shape of leaves, colour, size and arrangement of blossoms.

*Ligularia clivorum* is cultivated most frequently. The plant is about 1 metre (3 ft) high, with large, heart-shaped leaves. The blossoms are relatively large, 8 cms (3 ins) in diameter, golden-yellow to orange, on strong, branched stalks. They open in August and flower until September. There are several decorative varieties with large variously coloured blossoms and purple to red-brown leaves. The species *L. wilsoniana* is a larger plant with rounded, heart-shaped leaves. The light golden-yellow blossoms are more delicate and in a dense, long cluster. It flowers from September to October.

They grow best in a deep, humous soil, with sufficient moisture. They can be planted in damp places near water, ponds and streams, where they fit in beautifully with other damp- and shade-loving plants. All species also grow well in the sun, provided they have plenty of moisture.

They are propagated by division of the clumps in spring although the parent plants should not be too old. The plants will last for several years in one spot if looked after well. The planting distance is 80—100 cms (2½—3 ft).

*Ligularia clivorum*

## *Macleaya*
PLUME POPPY
180—250 cms (6—8 ft); VIII

Papaveraceae
The Poppy Family

Plume Poppy is a tall perennial, especially picturesque in its growth and foliage. It forms a clump of thin stalks with alternate broad, blue-green leaves which are divided by long notches into seven lobes, which are also indented. The stalk terminates in a plume of small fine blossoms, which are striking for the number of their stamens. The blossoms themselves are whitish and quite insignificant; the main beauty of the plant is in its foliage. The genus comes from Japan and China and in effect is cultivated in only one species, *Macleaya cordata*, which has small whitish blossoms. *M. c.* 'Kelway's Coral Plume' is a variety with reddish blossoms which form a good contrast with the blue-green leaves.

The Plume Poppy has no special requirements. It grows well in any garden soil, provided this is not too dry. It grows equally well in full sunshine or half-shade. It can be left in one place for years without much attention.

As a tall plant, it is appropriate for isolated groups set against a darker background in any large garden or park. It is sometimes invasive and this tendency can be prevented by inserting a piece of tin or tarred roof covering in the ground to obstruct it.

The plant forms underground offshoots, by which it is easily propagated in spring. The planting distance for the Plume Poppy is 60—80 cms (2—2½ ft).

*Macleaya cordata*

## *Kniphofia*
TORCH LILY,
RED HOT POKER
80—120 cms (2½—4 ft); VII—IX

Liliaceae
The Lily Family

The majority of species come from South Africa. These are interesting and attractive plants, forming tufts of long, narrow, backward-arching leaves, from which, in the flowering season, grow stalks more than 1 metre (3 ft) high terminating in thick spikes of tubular, drooping blossoms in brilliant colours.

Hybrid varieties are mainly cultivated. *Kniphofia hybrida* 'Bees Lemon' has golden-yellow blossoms and a height of 100 cms (3 ft) [VII—VIII]; *K. h.* 'Canary' has light yellow blossoms and a height of 80 cms (2½ ft) [VII—VIII]; *K. h.* 'Earliest of All' is orange and 70 cms (2¼ ft) high [VI—VII]; *K. h.* 'Indiana' is orange-red and 100 cms (3 ft) high [VII—VIII]; *K. h.* 'Orange Beauty' is shiny orange and 100 cms (3 ft) high [VII—VIII]; *K. h.* 'Maid of Orleans' is straw-coloured and 110 cms (3½ ft) tall [VIII—IX]; *K. h.* 'The Rocket' is a flaming red and 130 cms (4¼ ft) high [VII—IX].

The Torch Lilies grow best in a good well-drained, humous soil and in a sunny place. In spring they need a reasonable amount of moisture (and a feed with a liquid manure is also beneficial), but dry conditions in autumn and especially in winter. They can be killed by winter dampness, and should, therefore, be protected in winter by polythene and on top of that a covering of bracken.

The plant has an exotic appearance, and can be used anywhere. It is well suited to large groups in amongst low-growing perennials or grasses.

It is propagated by division in spring, and should be planted at intervals of 40 cms (16 ins).

*Kniphofia hybrida*

# *Rudbeckia*

CONEFLOWER

50—200 cms (1½—6½ ft); VIII—IX

Compositae
The Daisy Family

Coneflowers are one of the most important and ornamental of late-flowering perennials and for this reason are almost indispensable in the garden in late summer. There are many species, considerably different from each other and of varying decorative value. Some are small, while others are over 2 metres (6½ ft), but the small ones are the most useful. *Rudbeckia fulgida* 'Sullivantii' and the variety 'Goldsturm' are the most beautiful and most valuable of these. They form well-branched, bushy plants 50—60 cms (20—24 ins) high, with hairy, dark green, lanceolate leaves, and a number of large, golden-yellow blossoms, which have dark brown, raised centres. The plant is very compact and does not need staking. It is suitable not only as a smaller plant for separate beds, but also in mixed borders. It is especially effective in large groups.

Other Coneflowers are usually tall and have a lesser decorative value, but *R. nitida* at least must be mentioned. This is a tall species and its variety 'Herbstsonne' is usually grown. It is about 2 metres (6½ ft) high, with slightly divided, glossy deep green leaves. It forms tall bushy plants which flower profusely at the end of summer. The yellow blossoms are large, with broad, drooping petals and a large, nest-like, greenish-yellow cone. In spite of its considerable height this Coneflower is very firm and does not always need staking. It is used in large perennial groups.

Coneflowers grow well in any average garden soil as long as it is not too dry. *R. nitida* can also stand half-shade.

They are all propagated very easily by division of the tufts, best of all in spring. *R. fulgida* is planted 50 cms (20 ins) apart, *R. nitida* 80 cms (2½ ft) apart.

*Rudbeckia fulgida* 'Suilivantii'

## *Silene schafta*

CAMPION

10—20 cms (4—8 ins); VIII—IX

Caryophyllaceae

The Pink Family

This dwarf Campion comes from high altitudes in the Caucasus, but its appearance does not testify to this. It forms thin cushions of light green lanceolate leaves. In the flowering period (late summer), it is covered with star-shaped pink blossoms about 2 cms (¾ in.) across. It is a very valuable perennial because it flowers late, and by this time there are very few low-growing plants still in flower.

Well-drained, slightly alkaline or neutral soil is most suitable. The position should be sunny or even slightly overshadowed.

It is a useful perennial for rockeries, edgings and 'midget' borders among grey grasses *(Festuca, Avena)* and grey-leaved carpeting plants.

It is propagated easily by division and cuttings, and also from seed. The planting distance is 25 cms (10 ins).

*Silene schafta*

214

## *Aconitum*

Ranunculacea

MONKSHOOD

The Buttercup Family

100—150 cms (3—5 ft); VIII—X

The name of this genus is derived from the Greek word *akoniton* which, according to Dioscorides, is the name of the plant which was used for poisoning wolves and panthers. All species of Monkshood are poisonous.

They are medium-sized to rather tall plants with palmate, dark green leaves. The helmet-shaped blossoms are arranged in long spikes and their colour is usually blue to purple. Two species are mainly cultivated in gardens. The first is *Aconitum fischeri*, about 150 cms (5 ft) high, with light purple-blue flowers. It comes from eastern Asia. The second is *A. napellus* which is 100—150 cms (3—5 ft) high and flowers in July and August. It grows wild in both Europe and Asia. It is a plant typical of the banks of mountain streams and damp pastures at higher altitudes, 1,000—1,500 metres (3,000—4,500 ft). The blossoms are purple or blue. *A. napellus* has several decorative varieties, including a white form. Both species thrive best in half-shade, but if they have sufficient moisture, they will even grow in sunshine. *A. napellus* particularly needs dampness, while *A. fischeri* can stand drier conditions. The soil should be humous and loose.

It is used as a tall perennial to bring colour to the back of borders in late summer to autumn in combination with lighter-coloured perennials. It lasts many years in one place without special care. It can also be used for cutting, but care must be taken as the whole plant is poisonous.

It is propagated either by division of the fleshy roots in early spring soon after budding, or from seed. This should be sown in autumn, as germination is better from frozen seed. The seedlings should be transplanted and then moved to their final positions in August and September at intervals of 50 cms (20 ins).

*Aconitum fischeri*

# *Aster*

MICHAELMAS DAISY

Variable height; VIII—X

Composita

The Daisy Fami

Michaelmas Daisies have, perhaps, the widest range of colours
all autumn flowers. They are divided into several basic group
each of which has a number of varieties. The following thr
groups, each very rich in varieties, are the most important of t
taller Michaelmas Daisies.

*Aster amellus*, sometimes known as Italian Starwort, is t
earliest; it flowers from August to September and is 40—90 cm
(1¼—3 ft) high. The blossoms are in shades of blue, pink an
purple, and the leaves are covered with fine hairs. *A. a.* 'Herman
Löns' is silvery blue-purple and 60—70 cms (2—2¼ ft) high; *A.*
'Lady Hidlip' has large pink blossoms and is 60 cms (2 ft) hig
and *A. a.* 'Ultramarine' with dark purple blossoms is 50—60 cm
(1½—2 ft) high.

*Aster novae-angliae* is taller, about 120—150 cms (4—5 ft) an
flowers in September and October. The whole plant is hairy, an
the blossoms have delicate dense petals. *A. n.-a.* 'Constance' i
a dark blue-purple, semi-double variety, 120 cms (4 ft) high
*A. n.-a.* 'Harrington Pink' is a lively pink, semi-double an
120 cms (4 ft) high; *A. n.-a.* 'September Rubin' is dark carmine
red and 120 cms (4 ft) high.

*Aster novi-belgii* is 80—120 cms (2½—4 ft) high and flowers i
September. The plants have smooth stalks and leaves. They gliste
with shimmering colours ranging from white, purple, blue, pink
to shiny red. *A. n.-b.* 'Ernst Ballard' has large deep carmine-pink
blossoms and is 100 cms (3 ft) high; *A. n.-b.* 'Harrison's Blue' i
a double dark blue, 100 cms (3 ft) high; and *A. n.-b.* 'Winsto
Churchill' is a glowing red, 80 cms (2½ ft) high.

They grow best in a good light in well-drained soil. They ar
used for borders and for cutting. They are propagated mainly b
division of the tufts, and should be planted at intervals of 40 cm
(16 ins).

1. *Aster amellus* 'Hermann Löns'
2. *A. novae-angliae* 'Harrington Pink'
3. *A. novi-belgii* 'Winston Churchill

218

## *Helianthus*
SUNFLOWER
100—250 cms (3—8 ft); VIII—X

Composita
The Daisy Famil

Perennial Sunflowers are usually huge plants. They all have rough leaves and golden-yellow flowers with darker central disks varying in size. Four species are important in the garden. *Helianthus atrorubens* comes from the south-eastern part of North America. The tufts, about 180 cms (6 ft) high, have rough, wide lanceolate leaves. The flowers are golden-yellow, up to 18 cms (7 ins) in diameter, with darker disks. *H. decapetalus* is a perennial 100—120 cms (3—4 ft) high with yellow flowers; it flowers from July to August. It is cultivated mainly in its varieties, which are noted for their semi-double and double flowers. *H. salicifolius* is a species which forms tall, straight stalks, densely foliated from the ground upwards with narrow, willow-like leaves. The flowers are relatively small and appear at the end of September and in October. The attraction of this Sunflower lies in its growth and interesting foliage. *H. scaberrinus* is the last of the four and has many uses in the garden. It is a plant 100—150 cms (3—5 ft) high, indigenous to North America. The rough, lanceolate leaves are very broad and the blossoms are usually borne singly on the long stalks.

All Sunflowers need full sunshine and a nourishing soil. It is necessary to feed them occasionally and transplant them quite often. *H. salicifolius* is used as a very large foliage plant, whose tufts stand out nicely either as a solitary in the lawn or in groups near grasses and conifers. The other Sunflowers are good for cutting, for borders and in groups.

They are propagated by division or by cuttings. They should be planted at intervals of 70—80 cms (2¼—2½ ft).

*Helianthus salicifolius*

220

## *Acanthus*

BEAR'S BREECHES

100—150 cms (3—5 ft); IX—X

Acanthaceae

The Acanthus Family

Large, very ornate leaves are the main attraction of this large plant. In ancient Greece *Acanthus* leaves were used as a model for the capitals of Corinthian columns.

Of the number of possible species, *Acanthus mollis* is mainly chosen for garden cultivation. It forms a bulky basal rosette of large, beautifully shaped leaves, from which a stalk 1 metre (3 ft) high grows at the end of summer, bearing a huge spike of pinkish-white, double-lipped blossoms. *A. mollis latifolius* has broader and longer leaves and the flower spike is over 150 cms (5 ft) high.

Bear's Breeches requires a sunny position and grows in any ordinary garden soil. It will even grow in sandy soil, if it is improved with a good compost. All species are sensitive to winter dampness and also suffer considerably in abnormally wet years.

It is used mainly as a decorative solitary either individually or in groups. Smaller grasses *(Festuca, Avena)* and various sun-loving carpeting plants are its best companions.

It is propagated by careful division of the clump in spring, or by root cuttings in winter. It is also possible to propagate Bear's Breeches from seed. It should be planted at intervals of 60—80 cms ($2$—$2\frac{1}{2}$ ft).

*Acanthus mollis*

# *Aster dumosus*

DWARF MICHAELMAS
DAISY

20—60 cms (8—24 ins); IX—X

Compositae
The Daisy Family

Although there are quite a number of beautiful flowers still in bloom in early autumn, there are few low-growing species; dwarf Michaelmas Daisies are, therefore, particularly appreciated. The thick, dark green bushes when planted in large quantities form a continuous flowering carpet. They are covered with small blossoms in white, blue, pink and purple.

A number of varieties have been developed from the original North American species, of which many are invaluable for autumn displays in the garden.

*A. d.* 'Pink Lace' is a semi-double pink 30—40 cms (1—1¼ ft) high; *A. d.* 'Jenny' is a glowing reddish-purple 30 cms (1 ft) high; *A. d.* 'Lilac Time' is purple-blue, with delicate leaves and 40 to 50 cms (1¼—1½ ft) high; *A. d.* 'Little Red Boy' is a deep pink-red, flowers abundantly and is 40 cms (1¼ ft) high; *A. d.* 'Prof. A. Kippenburg' is a deep lavender-blue and *A. d.* 'Snowsprite' is a white, large-blossomed, early variety 23—30 cms (9—12 ins) high.

These *Asters* do not have any special requirements and grow well in any average garden soil, but they should have a sunny position if possible. To ensure a rich crop of flower every year, they should be left undisturbed for a long time in one place.

They can be used for formal bedding, for edging and for the front of the border. They also stand out well with clumps of red or yellow Chrysanthemums, with grasses and those shrubs and trees which have colourful autumn leaves or fruit.

They are propagated very easily by division; the best time to do this is in the spring. The planting distance is 30 cms (12 ins).

*Aster dumosus*

## *Chrysanthemum*

CHRYSANTHEMUM

40—100 cms (1¼—3 ft); IX—X

Compositae

The Daisy Family

Chrysanthemums have been developed into a number of beautiful
varieties of various forms and colours. Two species usually
dominate today's varieties: the single and double forms of
*Chrysanthemum indicum* which comes from China and Japan; and
from Korea, *Ch. koreanum*, with single blossoms similar to Ox-eye
Daisies. These garden Chrysanthemums have been recently de-
signated under one name, *Chrysanthemum × hortorum*. *Ch.× h.* 'Burgunder' is a wine-red, medium-sized variety; *Ch.× h.* 'White Wedg-
wood' is a pure white, semi-double, early variety about 80 cms
(2½ ft) high; *Ch.× h.* 'Apollo' is brick-red, single, early, and 70 cms
(2¼ ft) high; *Ch.× h.* 'Clara Curtis' is a glowing pink, single, early
variety which flowers profusely and is 60 cms (2 ft) high; *Ch.× h.*
'Duchess of Edinburgh' is a warm red, semi-double, early variety
70 cms (2¼ ft) high; *Ch.× h.* 'King Midas' is lemon-yellow, large,
double, medium early and 100 cms (3 ft) high; *Ch.× h.* 'Ruby King'
is a dark scarlet, full, medium early variety about 50—60 cms
(1½—2 ft) high.

Chrysanthemums need sun, a protected position and a good,
light, calcareous soil. Winter wet is harmful to them. In sheltered
positions during wet, warm weather, Chrysanthemums are easily
attacked by mildew.

Chrysanthemums, with Michaelmas Daisies and Japanese
Anemones, are the most beautiful and richly coloured autumn
perennials; they are most suitable for borders, for formal bedding
and for cutting. They are propagated by division or by putting
in new plants. They should be planted at intervals of 40—50 cms
(16—20 ins).

*Chrysanthemum × hortorum* 'Burgunder'

226

## *Artemisia*
SOUTHERNWOOD,
WORMWOOD
Variable height

Compositae
The Daisy Family

Southernwood is a well-known aromatic plant, often found growing wild on waste land. The genus has many species and some of them are important as decorative perennials. They are plants whose attraction mainly lies in their silvery foliage and habit of growth. They are, therefore, used mainly for forming colourful foliage effects.

*Artemisia lanata* is a very small plant, which forms thick cushions only 10—20 cms (4—8 ins) high; it is the most important of the low-growing species. Its drooping branches are covered with finely divided silvery leaves. The delicate greenish-grey blossoms are very insignificant, but there is no other creeping plant with such a silvery foliage.

It requires poor, sandy soil, best mixed with gravel. It must also have a dry, sunny position, and older plants should have the base of the stems covered with small stones, as damp conditions are very harmful to them. It is suitable for rockeries, dry walls and covering large areas and provides a ground-work for groups of perennials. It looks very attractive, especially when planted in association with grasses and variegated creepers. The planting distance is 20 cms (8 ins).

Of the taller species only *A. hybrida* 'Silver Queen' is mentioned here. It forms loose bushes, 70—80 cms (2¼—2½ ft) tall, of densely branched stems with silvery-grey leaves. The tiny blossoms are the same colour as the leaves. The decorative foliage of this bushy plant can be used as a feature in informal groups, especially in association with different darker creepers and grasses.

Both the above species are propagated by division in spring or by cuttings in summer. The planting distance for *A. h.* 'Silver Queen' is 50 cms (20 ins).

*Artemisia lanata*

## *Miscanthus sinensis*
EULALIA, ZEBRA GRASS
140—180 cms

Graminea
The Grass Famil

Decorative grasses play an important part in making a garde
attractive; above all they introduce lightness and delicacy c
foliage. *Miscanthus* is one of the most beautiful, valuable an
satisfying of all grasses.

*Miscanthus sinensis* var. *gracillimus* forms a clump 150 cms (5 ft
tall of long, narrow leaves, which droop slightly; when full-grown
it makes a beautiful garden feature. *M. s.* var. *variegatus* has broade
leaves, with yellow-white edges. The plant is about 150 cms (5 ft
high and its leaves arch downwards beautifully, giving the plan
a special charm. *M. s.* var. *zebrinus* has a rather stiff, upright growt
and wider leaves with transverse yellow stripes. This leaf colourin
is very interesting, unusual and attractive. The plant reache
a height of up to 180 cms (6 ft).

All the species mentioned need a good, deep, porous and well
drained garden soil. They require plenty of moisture in spring bu
dry conditions in winter. They prefer sunny positions but can als
stand light half-shade. In spring, after removing the protectiv
winter covering, the dead stalks should be cut down.

*Miscanthus* is usually planted as a solitary. Small groups placec
in the lawn or near stretches of water are very decorative, but i
should be remembered that dry conditions are essential in winter
In small gardens these grasses are beautiful near seats, walls, stone
ornaments, etc.

It is propagated by division in spring. The divisions should no
be too small, or it will take a long time for the plant to mature
The planting distance is 60—80 cms (2—2½ ft).

*Miscanthus sinensis* var. *zebrinu*

230

# INDEX

233

234